LITTLE TORA

THE SWEDISH SCHOOLMISTRESS

And Other Stories

MRS. WOODS BAKER

1st WORLD
LIBRARY
Literary Society

Little Tora, The Swedish Schoolmistress

Mrs. Woods Baker

© 1st World Library, 2008
PO Box 2211
Fairfield, IA 52556
www.1stworldlibrary.com
First Edition

LCCN: 2007935426

Softcover ISBN: 978-1-4218-9377-8
Hardcover ISBN: 978-1-4218-9477-5
eBook ISBN: 978-1-4218-9277-1

Purchase *"Little Tora, The Swedish Schoolmistress"*
as a traditional bound book at:
www.1stWorldLibrary.com/purchase.asp?ISBN=978-1-4218-9377-8

1st World Library is a literary, educational organization
dedicated to:

- Creating a free internet library of downloadable ebooks

- Hosting writing competitions and offering book publishing
scholarships.

Interested in more 1st World Library books? contact:
literacy@1stworldlibrary.com
Check us out at: www.1stworldlibrary.com

1st World Library Literary Society

Giving Back to the World

"If you want to work on the core problem, it's early school literacy."

- James Barksdale, former CEO of Netscape

"No skill is more crucial to the future of a child, or to a democratic and prosperous society, than literacy."

- Los Angeles Times

"Literacy... means far more than learning how to read and write... The aim is to transmit... knowledge and promote social participation."

- UNESCO

"Literacy is not a luxury, it is a right and a responsibility. If our world is to meet the challenges of the twenty-first century we must harness the energy and creativity of all our citizens."

- President Bill Clinton

"Parents should be encouraged to read to their children, and teachers should be equipped with all available techniques for teaching literacy, so the varying needs and capacities of individual kids can be taken into account."

- Hugh Mackay

CONTENTS

A SWEDISH SCHOOLMISTRESS

A WEEK AT KULLEBY

ALF

LITTLE TORA: THE SWEDISH SCHOOLMISTRESS

CHAPTER I

LITTLE TORA

The kindly doctor was entertaining his brother-in-law, and all the family were sitting round the table in state. The polished silver and shining glass, with porcelain, flowers, and fruit, seemed to be all that had been provided for the dinner.

The usual "grace" had hardly been said, when a trim maid announced that a little girl was at the door, who must see the doctor about something particular. "There is nobody sick more than usual," she says; "but she must come in," continued the irritated damsel-in-waiting.

"Let her come in here. You can never have your meals in peace!" said the doctor's wife affectionately.

The soup and the little girl came in together, the latterly evidently quite prepared to state her errand. She was a small, straight child, with a determined air and a cheery face, as if sure of success in her undertaking. Fresh in Monday cleanliness, her white cotton head-kerchief stood stiffly out in a point behind, and her calico apron was without spot or wrinkle. Her shoes, though they had been diligently blackened and were under high polish, did not correspond with the rest of her appearance. They had evidently been made for a boy, an individual much larger than their present wearer. Great wrinkles crossing each other shut off some low, unoccupied land near the toe, and showed how much of the sole had been too proud to touch the common ground. All this the observers saw at once.

"Well, Tora!" said the doctor pleasantly, after she had dropped her bob-courtesies, and "good-days" had been exchanged.

"May I sing for you?" said the little girl, without further hesitation, as she hastily took out a thin, black book from the small pocket handkerchief in which it had been carefully wrapped.

"Sing? yes, surely!" said the doctor. "Just the thing for us while we are taking our dinner. My brother-in-law here is a famous judge of music, so you must do your best."

Tora opened the book, took what she considered an imposing position, and announced the name of the song. It was a patriotic one, and in the full chorus of the schoolroom it had stirred the young Swedish hearts to their depths.

The first few notes were right, though tremblingly given; then came a quivering and a faltering and a falsity that made the doctor's boys cover their laughing mouths with their hands, while their eyes twinkled with suppressed merriment.

Just then there was a queer buzzing noise in the room, by which the tune was carried on, and Tora fell in with fresh courage. Most of the party were taking their soup, as well as listening; but the boys observed that their uncle quietly held his motionless spoon, and was looking at the singer as if lost in musical bliss. His mouth was closed, but his nostrils seemed undergoing a rhythmical contraction and distension most interesting and unusual.

Tora gave the closing notes in fine style, and the expression of applause was general. So encouraged, she volunteered a simple newly-published carol that she had that day been practising at school. Here it seemed the musical accompaniment could not be relied upon. Tora began, stopped, and began again, then was silent, while great tears stood in her eyes.

One of the before-smiling boys hastened to say,—

"Let her speak a piece, uncle. She can do that beautifully, her brother Karl says. He has taught her ever so many, and it costs her nothing to learn them. He likes to tell that she is the best scholar in her class."

The uncle seemed to be able to enjoy his dinner at the same time as the elocutionary treat with which it was now accompanied, and he warmly complimented the speaker on her performance at its close.

"What made you think of giving us this pleasure, little Tora?" said the doctor, with a humorous look in his kindly face.

"Why," said the little girl at once, "I don't like my shoes. They have been brother Karl's. When I asked father this morning to give me some new ones, he said this was a fine strong pair and did not let in water, and he could not think of letting them go to waste. Then he looked sorrowful, and I heard him say to mother, 'The poor children will have to earn all they have soon.' I made up my mind to begin at once, and earn my shoes, if I could. Our teacher told us to-day about Jenny Lind, who began to sing when she was a very little girl, and when she was older she made a great deal of money, and gave away ever so much, and was loved and admired wherever she went. I thought I should like to be loved and admired wherever I went, and have new shoes whenever I wanted them, and I would try singing too. I came here first because the doctor has always been so pleasant to me and so good to us all."

"You have made a real beginning," said the brother-in-law.—"Gustaf, take round the hat."

The doctor's son ran for his cap. There was a chinking and a silver flash as the uncle put his hand into the cap. Something of the same kind happened when it came to the doctor's turn to contribute. The mother fumbled confusedly in her pocket, and found only her handkerchief. The boys tossed in conspicuously some coppers of their own, perhaps with the idea of covering, by their munificence, the evident discomfiture of their mother.

"There! there!" said the uncle. "Hand the cap to the little girl. What is in it is for the singer. As for the shoes, I'll see about that.—I would not advise you, though, little Tora, to try singing to make money. It might do for Jenny Lind, but I hardly think it would suit for you."

The little girl's countenance fell. The friendly stranger went on, "How would you like to be a little schoolmistress? That would be a nice way for you to take care of yourself, and maybe help all at home, by-and-by. I know how that thing is done, and I think we could manage it."

The uncle did know "how that thing was done," and who meant to do it. Little Tora was provided for from that day;

and so, if she did not sing like Jenny Lind, she sang herself into being a schoolmistress—a little schoolmistress of the very best order.

CHAPTER II

FACING THE WORLD

It was five o'clock in the morning on one of the last days of August. This was no legally-sanctioned Swedish moving-day, and yet it was plain that with somebody a change of residence was in progress.

Before a low house on a winding "cobble-stone" paved street two long, narrow wagons were standing. Their horses faced in different directions, though in all other respects the two establishments were, even to their loading, like a pair of twins. In each was the furniture for one simple room, a sofa-bed being the striking article in the inventory. A carefully-packed basket of china, a few primitive cooking utensils, and some boxes and packages indicated, if not good cheer, at least something to keep soul and body together.

The outer door of the house was locked at last, and the key had been handed to a humble woman, who courtesied and took it as a matter of form; though both parties knew that she would soon be opening that door and coming into lawful possession of all the effects, remnants, and refuse left on the premises, and would be sure to hand that house over to the landlord in a superlatively clean and tidy condition.

Two stout men took their places as drivers, and two passengers stood on the low steps for a few parting words. They were by no means twins. The straight, slight girl, though not tall, yet fully grown, had been the little Tora, the singer of one public performance. Now she had in her pocket her greatest treasure—the paper that pronounced her a fully-fledged schoolmistress; who had completed with honour the prescribed course at the seminary duly authorized for the manufacture of teachers of unimpeachable character, and all pedagogical requisites in perfection.

At Tora's side stood "brother Karl," just about to start for Upsala University, with his arrangements complete for his bachelor housekeeping on the most simple principles.

There was no effusiveness in the parting. "Keep well, Karl, and don't study too hard," said the sister. "And don't have any 'food-days'; I could not bear that. But you must not live too low, and pull yourself down. Send to me if you get to the bottom of your purse. I shall be likely to have a few coppers in mine."

"I'll warrant that, Miss Prudence," was his reply. "Nobody but you would have managed to keep us both comfortably on what was only meant to carry you through the seminary. Don't be afraid for me! I shall clear my own way. I shall teach boys in the evening, and study after they have gone to bed. I have served a good apprenticeship with the doctor's chaps these years. I understand packing lessons into youngsters to be given out in the class next day. Then I am to write an article now and then for the paper here, with Upsala news for the country folks. As to 'food-days,' I am not exactly of your mind. I have made arrangements for one already."

"O Karl! how could you?" said Tora reproachfully.

"Gunner Steelhammer liked well enough to take porridge with us now and then when he was teaching here. His mother has told him to invite me to dine at their house on Sundays, and to call there whenever I feel like it. We are real friends, though he is a university tutor now. Anybody that I would be willing to help I am willing to let help me. Of course, I shall enjoy a good substantial dinner once a week, but I really care more to be with the family at that house. Gunner is a splendid fellow, as you know, and his father draws all kinds of nice people about him, I hear. I did not dare to tell you this before, little sister; but now I have made a clean breast of it. I was half teasing about it, too. Be sure, I'll work hard and live low before I shall let anybody help me. Well, good-bye," and he stretched out his hand to Tora, who took it hastily for a hearty shake, and then they parted.

Karl was wearing his white university cap, which, with the loading of the wagon, marked him as a student on the way to Upsala, and would ensure him many a friendly greeting by the way. Tora had prudently covered the fresh velvet with a fair cotton cover; but the blue-and-yellow rosette was in full sight—a token of the honours he had lately won at his examination, and would be striving to win at the old centre of learning. The kind neighbours whom he had known from boyhood had added to his equipment—here a cheese, and there a pat of butter or a bag of fresh biscuits; but he did not need to open his stores by the way. Now and again from the roadside houses kindly faces smiled on him, and homely fare was offered him by the elders; while flowers or wild berries came to his share from glad children who had been ranging the woods for treasures during these last days of their summer vacation.

As for Tora, sitting in a low chair in the midst of her posses-sions, she went rattling over the cobble-stones, if not more proud at least more happy of heart than a conqueror of old at

Mrs. Woods Baker

the head of a Roman triumph. She had reached the goal towards which she had long been striving. She was now an independent worker, with a profession by which she could earn an honourable living. She was a teacher, "a teacher of the little school"—that is to say, of the school for little children. The state was her sure paymaster. If continued health were granted her, her path for the future was plain— her bread was sure.

The cobble-stones were soon passed, and over the smooth country road rumbled the clumsy vehicle, now through evergreen thickets, now through groves of bright birches, and at last out on the rolling meadows. The fences had disappeared, and but for a lone landmark here and there, the sea of green might have seemed the property of any strong-handed labourer who might choose to call it his own.

Down an unusually steep slope the wagon passed, then across the low meadow with a bright stream threading its midst, and then there was a triumphant sweep up to the little red schoolhouse where Tora was to have her abode and the sphere of her labours.

A low wooded point ran like a promontory out into the meadow, and there "the forefathers of the vale" had built the temple for the spelling-book and the slate.

On the opposite side from the meadow the schoolhouse was entered, after crossing the wide playground. Where "the field for sport" ended at the road there stood a lad, evidently looking out eagerly for the arrival of the new teacher.

"That's a life-member of the little school," said the driver, with a whimsical look. "Nils is not much at books, but he's a powerful singer."

The last words were spoken within the hearing of the frank-faced boy, who now pulled off his cap, and stepped up to the wagon to help Tora down. She shook his hand kindly, and said, "I hear you are a singer, Nils. I am glad of that, for in my certificate I got but a poor record for my singing."

"And 'great A' for everything else, mother said," he answered promptly, while his eyes beamed pleasantly on the new teacher, whose first friendly greeting had won his heart.

"I'll help you down with the heavy things first," said Nils to the driver, "and then if you'll set the rest here, we'll take them in together later. I want to show the schoolhouse to the mistress."

The one room set apart for the home of the teacher did not look dreary as she stepped into it. The table from the school-room stood in the centre covered with a white cloth, its edge outlined by bright birch leaves laid on it, loosely and taste-fully, like a wreath. Then on a tray covered with a snowy napkin stood a shining coffee-pot, with cups for three, and a light saffron cake that might have sufficed for the whole school assembled.

"Mother thought perhaps you would like a taste of something warm after your ride," said Nils, as he proceeded to pour out a cup of coffee as if he were quite at home. At home he was in a way, for in that schoolhouse he had for years passed his days among the little ones, through a special permit from the school board.

Tora clasped her hands, and stood silent a moment before she tasted the first morsel of food in her new home, and her heart sent up really grateful thoughts to her heavenly Father, who had so blessed her, and would, she was sure, continue to bless her in her new surroundings.

"May I take out a cup to Petter?" asked Nils, while he cut the big cake into generous pieces, and offered the simple entertainment to the teacher. Of course the driver did not refuse the proposed refreshment, nor did Nils hesitate to help himself, while the mistress was taking her coffee and glancing round the premises.

All was fresh and clean about her. The windows had evidently been open since early morning, and the closets and shelves could well afford to be displayed through the doors more than half ajar.

"Thanks, Nils," said the mistress, as she took the boy's hand after the refreshment.

"Thanks and welcome to the new teacher!" was the reply.

"Now I shall go in and look at the schoolroom while Petter and you furnish my room for me. The sofa should stand there, and the bureau there. The rest I can leave to you," said Tora, as she disappeared.

Nils unfolded a strip of rag carpeting and "criss-crossed" it round the room, whispering to himself, "Mother said there were to be no footmarks left behind us."

The schoolroom was but a big, bare room—no maps on the walls, none of the modern aids for instruction, save that the space between the two windows that looked out towards the meadow had been painted, to be used as a blackboard: "a useless, new-fangled notion" the rustics had called this forward step in the way of education.

In front of the blackboard stood a wooden armchair for the teacher. The benches were low, and the desks were of the simplest sort, saving one, which was larger and higher, which the teacher at once understood was the permanent arrangement for Nils. Her heart went out towards the big, kind fellow, on whom so sore a trial had been laid in his youth.

Along one side of the schoolroom there were four horses standing silent, but not "saddled and bridled," as in old nursery stories. Without head or tail, they stood on four sprawling legs—supports for two long, "shallow boxes" that had been in the schoolroom for fifty years or more. Wood was abundant in the old days, and unskilful hands had done the work; so the boxes were but clumsy specimens of carpentry, and deep enough, it seemed, to hold sand for all the long winter through. The grandfathers of the neighbourhood could remember when these receptacles were their writing-desks, in which, stick in hand, they were taught to trace in the smoothed sand their names or any higher efforts of chirography that the teacher might demand. These superannuated articles of furniture were now used in winter as places of deposit for the children's folded outer garments, rather than the cold vestibule. There, too, the dinner-baskets had their rightful quarters.

The room was high, as it went up to the very roof. On the rafters were stored, in cold weather, the stilts for summer, and the bundles of ropes for the swings to be fastened to the tall trees by adventurous Nils, whose friendly hands delighted to send the laughing little ones flying far up into the fresh air like merry fairies. There, too, were the bows and arrows, and all other lawful things for summer sport.

The little schoolmistress took a full survey of her new kingdom, sat for a moment in her chair of state, and noticed a simple footstool put in front of it for her use, as she fancied, by that unknown "mother" who seemed to have her comfort so much at heart.

When the new mistress returned to her own private apartment, the furniture was all in place, the covers were taken from the boxes, and everything was ready for her personal arrangement of her property.

"The school board have had shutters put to the windows," said the driver, pointing to the late improvement. "They thought perhaps the new teacher might be afraid. This is a lonely place."

"Afraid!" said the little schoolmistress, wonderingly; "I am never afraid, night or day."

The driver opened his eyes wide as he answered,—

"The last teacher was as tall as I am, and she always kept a pistol at night by her on a chair, with an apron thrown over it, so the thieves could not find it and shoot her before she had a chance at them. This little mistress must be made of different stuff.—Well, good-bye, miss, and I wish you well."

Tora was about to put in his hand the usual payment for his services, when he shut his broad fist expressively, and then half raised it, as he said,—

"I never took pay for a mistress's things being brought to this schoolhouse yet, and I don't mean to do it now. Folks for the most part seem to like you, but I have a particular feeling. I knew your father once, and he was good to me."

The honest man could say no more just then, and he hurried out of the room. Nils followed with his best bow, but the pleasant words reached his ears,—

"We'll meet soon again. Thanks! thanks to you both.—I think we shall be real friends, Nils, you and I."

That little allusion to her father, coming so suddenly, had almost made Tora break down in the midst of her abounding courage. The past came up in vivid pictures where scenes of sorrow were predominant. Her weak, ever-ailing little baby sister had floated quietly across the dark river. The stricken mother sank, and soon followed her child to the churchyard. The father's hand, that had first guided an editor's pen, and then in his long decline that of a mere copyist, grew weaker and weaker, and finally the last loving pressure was given to his daughter, and then that hand lay still and white. Its work on earth was done, and the brother and sister were left alone. Courageous and loving, they had both struggled on. Her end was attained, but he was at the beginning of the steady conflict before him. How would he bear himself in the battle? If she could only know whether his surroundings would be as pleasant and homelike as her own, and his heart as full of hope and quiet trust! Would he be borne safely through the privations and temptations of his university life? A prayer went silently up to the Father of all for that absent brother, and then the practical little sister was soon deep in the stir of bringing all things to order in her new home. Physical effort brought back the resolute cheerfulness so natural to the little schoolmistress, and she hummed to herself a simple song of long ago, to which she could always hear the buzzing accompaniment of that stranger who had proved to her a faithful, untiring benefactor and friend.

Mrs. Woods Baker

CHAPTER III

A NARROW ESCAPE

The winter had been unusually long. For nearly six months the ground had been continually white. Not that it had been clothed by an ever-smooth, fair mantle. The snow had been tossed and whirled by the wild winds till it was fitfully heaped, now in the meadows, and now banked up against the very hill-sides. But for the dark woods as landmarks, the face of the country would have seemed to be utterly changed. The ice-covered streams were hidden away out of sight, and the wide ponds appeared but as smooth pastures.

A path from the little-frequented road had been kept open to the schoolhouse. Week by week this narrow way to the seat of learning had been walled higher and higher, until at last the rustic scholars seemed passing through a stately white marble corridor as they filed along towards the well-known door.

The first days of April had come and gone without a flower-bud to greet them. The weather had suddenly grown soft and mild, and a drizzling rain had been falling all night.

Nils appeared early at school; but the tidy mistress had already cleared away all traces of her modest breakfast, and was ready to bid him welcome more as a visitor than a scholar. They had some pleasant chat together, and then the teacher said seriously, as she laid her hand on the boy's shoulder, "You must try as hard as you can, Nils, to do well, or I am afraid you will not 'go up' this year."

"I do try—I try as hard as I can!" he said. Tears suddenly filled his large eyes as he added, "I am not like other boys, and I know it."

"God knows what you can do, Nils," she said tenderly; "and He will not judge you for what is not your fault. It may be, 'Well done, good and faithful servant!' for you at the last, if you cannot be a great scholar."

Some merry voices at the door put an end to the conversation, and the school was soon going on in its usual routine.

Many weather-wise mothers had kept their children at home, and only eight scholars were in their places, not counting Nils, who occupied in many practical things a middle ground between the little ones and the teacher.

A heavy rain soon began to fall, and pattered cheerily on the roof, to the great delight of the small pupils. Towards noon the schoolmistress was hearing the class read aloud. She sat with her back to the windows, with the light falling on the book she held in her hand; but she did not see a letter. Suddenly she looked up and said, "Nils, please open the right-hand shutter in my room."

The boy obeyed instantly; but in another moment he said quickly, "Please come in here a moment, teacher."

She disappeared immediately, closing the door behind her. Nils pointed to the window with wide-open eyes, and said,

Mrs. Woods Baker

"The meadow is all afloat!"

"I know it!" she answered calmly. "I saw it while the children were getting their books for the class. If the pond above breaks over the banks, we may be all swept away in a moment. There is no time to be lost. The children must not be frightened. I have thought just what to do. You can swim, Nils?"

"Yes," was his only answer.

"I can swim too," she said. "If anything goes wrong, we must do what we can for the children." She looked into the clear, calm eyes of the boy, and she knew she could trust him. They returned quietly to the schoolroom. The teacher had hardly taken her seat and closed the book she had held in her hand, when there was a loud crashing sound without, and a heavy thud against the outer door.

"It's all right," said Nils calmly, taking his cue from the teacher. "I put up the bar after the children came in. I supposed this might happen."

"We don't mind the snow falling against the door," said the teacher cheerfully. "We didn't mean to go out that way. We shall go home by boat anyhow. I've thought about that before."

"By boat!" exclaimed the children delightedly, for to them a row or a sail was the most charming thing in the world.

"But where's the boat?" asked a prudent little boy, with a sceptical look in his small countenance. "And where's the water?" he would have added if he had dared.

"Two boats—two boats are here! I see them now!" said the

teacher, glancing at the sand-boxes.—"Nils, climb up into the rafters and bring down the oars."

Climbing to the rafters was a familiar exploit of Nils's. With one foot on his desk and his knee to the wall, he swung himself up in a moment.

"Hand down my oars and yours," she said, as she pointed at the stilts; for the little schoolmistress was a leader in the sports of her children, and often enjoyed them as much as they did.

The stilts were duly secured, and then the order followed, "And now the ropes for the launching," and another glance prompted the lowering of the summer swings for their new use.

"Give out the clothes, Nils, and call the names of the children as usual," said the teacher. Those were no dainty little ones, accustomed to be dressed like passive dolls by careful nurses or over-fond mammas. They had but to receive their garments in the daily orderly way, and to put them on as they well knew how. There might sometimes be an obstinate string or button, but Nils was sure to be able to help in any such difficulty, or even to tie a refractory kerchief over the light locks. The children now put on their wrappings mechanically, lost in watching the proceedings of the teacher and her obedient assistant.

The swings were cut in halves and attached to the strong handles of the empty sand-boxes of olden times. "And now we must launch the boats," said the teacher, with the nearest approach she could muster to the manner of a bluff sea-captain.

"Heave ho!" shouted Nils, as he put his strong shoulders to

the work of moving the boats, while the mistress held on to the horses.

One by one the boats were put in what Tora deemed proper position, the square prows curiously tilted up to the broad window-seat. Then came the orders—"Climb to the top of the shutter, Nils! Pass that rope round the upper hinge; tie it fast! Now the other rope on the lower hinge. Right! The same with the other ropes—bind them fast to the other shutter-hinges!"

Every order was promptly and skilfully obeyed.

"Nils, are you sure the boats are perfectly watertight?" said the mistress, with, for the first time, a shadow of anxiety in her determined face.

"Tight as a bottle!" was the immediate reply. "We had them filled with water for the last examination, to float the boats the children had made. The ships and such like were here, and the row-boats and canoes in the other."

"I saw them! I saw them all!" exclaimed a little chap, with great delight. "My brother had the prize for his ship, and he made it every bit himself." The eager memories that came to the minds of the children were chatted about with an intensity that made the boats of the moment to be almost for the time forgotten.

Now came the real launching of the boats. With a proper amount of drawing in and letting out and holding fast on the part of Nils and the teacher, the long boxes sat at last on the water like a pair of contented swans.

"Get down into the boat you are to be captain of, and I will hand down the oars for us both. Lay mine across my boat and yours across yours. Your passengers are to come down first. There will be four for each of us."

The little schoolmistress, putting on her coat and fur cap, backed up to one of her little girls, saying, "Put your arms round my neck, and you shall ride to the boat."

Two chubby arms went willingly round the neck of the teacher, as they had done many a time before on a less momentous occasion. So the little one, with her eyes away from the window, was backed up to it, to be lifted down by Nils with a merry shout as he landed the first passenger. The others followed in the same style, and all the eight were cheerily deposited in high good-humour.

"Now I'll come down, too," said the schoolmistress, and she came down the rope as if she were in a gymnasium. She took her place in the centre of her boat, with two delighted children before her and two more behind her.

"Cut loose, Nils! One rope as long as you can, and the other short up to the stern; and then give me your knife, and I'll do the same for mine. Now start, Nils! I'll follow."

The orders were rapidly given and promptly obeyed, and then the little party started across the watery stretch that had taken the place of the meadow.

Nils, with his strong arms, got on rapidly, and his boat was soon far in advance of the other. He neared the bank, plunged in and drew the uncertain little craft to the shore, and then as a sledge up the long slope.

Nils had before decided that he would deposit his passengers in a sheepfold high on the bank, where he had seen in the morning a window left open under the projecting roof to give

Mrs. Woods Baker

the poor creatures a little air. He knew that in the corner by the window there was a great bin that had been freshly filled with dried birch branches as food for the sheep. He left the children looking down at the pretty lambs and their mothers, and ran back himself to see what he could do for the rest of the party.

The little mistress was only half-way over, and evidently managing with difficulty her awkward oars in the thick, snow-encumbered water through which she was making her way.

Nils plunged in, swam to her boat, tied the loose rope round his body, and then struck out for the shore, while the oars were plied as well as they could be by the weary hands that held them. His feet had just touched bottom when there was a loud cheer from the top of the hill that sloped down to the meadow. Two great wagons, with a pair of strong horses attached to each, were coming to the rescue of the children.

As horses that were good forders and wagons suited to the purpose were to be selected, some time had been lost in the preparations after the first news of the condition of the meadow had been spread abroad. The question now was how to get the whole party under roof as soon as possible.

The drivers were for putting the children half in one wagon and half in the other; but Nils said in a tone most unusual for him, "*All* the children must go in one wagon, and you will see them safe home, Petter. *We* go the other way where the road forks. Of course, I take the mistress home with me. Mother wouldn't forgive me if I let her go anywhere else; and I think I have a kind of right to her too!"

"That you have," said the rough man, with a kind of little quiver round his lips. "You've earned that right, anyhow."

And away Nils and the teacher were borne, while from the other wagon there was a merry "Good-bye! good-bye! good-bye, teacher! good-bye, Nils!" and a hearty shout of "Hurrah for Nils!" from the driver, which came from the very depths of Petter's honest heart.

Mrs. Woods Baker

CHAPTER IV

A HAPPY MORNING

The home to which the little schoolmistress and Nils were bound had formerly been a wayside inn of most modest pretensions. It was but a one-story red building, with a row of white-framed windows looking out on the road close at hand. There was a storm-house, for stamping off the snow and depositing extra articles of carriage, and for dogs, who, like the Peri, must stand outside the paradise within. Next came one large, cheerful room, which served as kitchen, as well as general place of refreshment and assembly. On one side of this apartment of manifold uses were four small rooms for lodgers, furnished with almost as much simplicity as the prophet's chamber of the Scriptures, save that a plain sofa-bed was added in each, as a possible accommodation for an extra sleeper when there was a throng of guests.

On the death of Nils's father, the widow had resolved to retire into private life, as she was comfortably provided for. Not but that she was willing at times to give a meal or a bed to an old acquaintance; but such inmates must conform to the temperance arrangements of the establishment, for total abstinence was now the rule of the house. The widow had declared that her son should not be brought up with the fumes of spirituous liquors as his natural atmosphere.

Perhaps this resolution had been prompted by the suspicion that her husband's life had been shortened by too frequent good meals and too frequent strong potations. Be that as it may, the determined woman had made it known that, now that she was mistress in her own house, she would manage it as she thought best. The tables for guests had been swept away (or rather sold discreetly at private sale) to make room for a spinning-wheel, a loom, and a sewing-machine, by which the prudent woman said she was sure she could add to her substance in a quiet way. "The clicking, the buzzing, and the slamming," she said, were nothing to her, and now she could choose what noises she would have in her ears.

It was not yet time for the usual return of her son from school, but the mother had begun to go to the door to see if Nils could possibly be coming. Perhaps the old habit of looking out occasionally up and down the road, to reconnoitre as to what customers might be expected, had lingered to keep the former hostess now constantly, as it were, on guard. In one of these excursions for inspection she was surprised to see a big wagon drawing up before the door, with the schoolmistress and Nils as passengers.

The driver hastened to tell in an abridged form the story of their experiences, and to hand over his charge, with as many orders that they should be well looked after as if he were the only person interested in the matter.

The doors to the little bedrooms were always kept ajar when unoccupied, that they might be at least not chilly when needed. Two of them were immediately put into requisition. Nils, as in the most desperate case, was stripped and rubbed down, and put into bed at once; and then the little schoolmistress was looked after. She had obeyed orders, and her pale face lay on the pillow when she was visited. The quondam hostess left her suddenly, and soon returned with a hot drink, which she assured the patient would make her "quite natural." To Nils a similar draught was administered, with the command that he should dash it down at once, with "no sipping," and go to sleep afterwards.

"Wasn't that whisky?" exclaimed Nils, in surprise.

"There *was* a drop in it," owned the mother; adding, "I would give it clear to anybody dying. I am not wild crazy about temperance, boy."

"Do you think I am dying?" said Nils; and then he hastily added, "I should not like to leave you and the schoolmistress; but for anything else I should not mind. Maybe I should be like other folks up there."

"Hush, child! You are not dying, nor likely to be; you are as strong as a bear. A little dip in cold water is not going to hurt you. That stuff has gone to your head and made you melancholy-like and weepish. It does sometimes; it don't generally, though, just in a minute. You go to sleep; and don't let me hear anything from you for one while."

The mother put down the thick paper shade, and set a pin here and there along the edge, to keep out any adventurous rays of light that might be peeping in at the sleeper—"a pin practice" she had sorely complained of when ventured upon by restless lodgers. The same process was gone through in the room where the mistress was lying. The locks and hinges of the doors were carefully oiled, and then the agitated woman sat down to meditate and be thankful. The meditation proved to be of the perambulatory sort, for she peeped into one room and then into the other, noiselessly appearing and retiring. She listened to see if her patients were alive. The schoolmistress lay pale and still; her hands, loosely spread out, dropped on the sheet almost as colourless as itself. But she breathed regularly; that was an ascertained fact. Nils was frequently visited. He gave audible tokens as to how he was enjoying himself. The mother sat down for the fifth or sixth time, as it might be, in the great, quiet room. She did not enter upon any of her favourite branches of home industry; she thought them too noisy for the occasion. She was not a reader. She could but nod a little in her chair, and then make another round of observation.

At last, towards evening, the schoolmistress was fairly awake; and such a dish of porridge as she was obliged to consume! Such a series of inquiries she was subjected to as to her symptoms and sensations as would have done credit to a young medical practitioner examining his first patient, though the questions, in this case, were practically rather than scientifically put, and could actually be understood by the respondent.

To have quiet was all that the little schoolmistress craved, and that she was at last allowed. As for Nils, it was plain that he considered that small apartment his sleeping-car, for which his ticket had been taken for the livelong night.

The schoolmistress rose early. Her room was soon in perfect order. She was reading devoutly in the Bible: that had been an accessory in the arrangement of her room, as of all the other small dormitories, since the hostess "had her way in her own house."

Tora suddenly heard a quick repeated knock at her door. The permission to enter was hardly given when Nils burst in, his face glowing with delight.

"It's all right with me, teacher!" he exclaimed—"it's all right with me! You know that hymn I've tried to learn so many times, and couldn't make out. The first line came into my head yesterday in our troubles—'God is our stronghold and defence;' but I could not get any further."

"Perhaps that was far enough just then, Nils," said Tora. "I thought of that line too myself when I first suspected how matters stood, as I sat there with my book before me."

"But, teacher, I'm all right. This morning I thought I would read that hymn all over, and I did—twice. And then, O teacher, I'm all right, for the whole hymn just repeated itself in my mind as if I had the book before me. I asked mother to hear me, and when she saw I could say it all through without a stumble, she put her arms round my neck and cried and talked about herself dreadfully. She said she had been such a sinner to make prayers and never believe they could come true; and that she hadn't taken any comfort, either, in what the doctor had always been telling her, and that she had thought was awful. He had said that if anything remarkable could happen to me, or any great shock, or even if I had a hard blow on the head, I might come round like other boys. She had felt sure that nothing remarkable could ever happen to me; and as to anybody's giving me a hard knock on the head, she would not have let that happen when she was by. She said she had prayed and worried, and never thought of leaving it all to her heavenly Father, and now she wasn't fit to have such a blessing. I couldn't make her glad about it; but she'll come round, I'm sure, teacher, if you'll just go and talk to her."

The teacher's eyes were full of tears of joy as she took Nils by the hand and said, "You are all right, I really believe. May God bless you, and make you a good and useful man."

The mother was not to be found. She was locked into her own room. There she was pouring out thanksgiving from the depths of her heart now for the first time in her life, understanding that she had indeed a loving heavenly Father, and that even her faithlessness and ingratitude could be forgiven.

It was a happy morning at the wayside inn.

Mrs. Woods Baker

CHAPTER V

THE PERMANENT PUPIL

The dear old schoolhouse had been swept away in the destructive flood that followed but ten minutes after the escape of the little schoolmistress with her pupils.

Intense gratitude for the happy deliverance of the children spread through the neighbourhood. A public meeting was called, where the thanks of the community were conveyed by a dignified and most complimentary spokesman, to the blushing confusion of Tora and the astonishment of Nils that he was said to have behaved so remarkably well on the memorable occasion. Of course, the newspapers throughout the country celebrated the praises of the little schoolmistress, and to the meeting in her honour came her friends from far and near. "Brother Karl" and his devoted Gunner made a point of being present, and Tora's buzzing benefactor beamed on the occasion, as if the credit were all his own.

That there must be a new schoolhouse was a self-evident fact. It was built as promptly as possible. The admirable building, with all its modern aids and appurtenances, was not placed on the old site, but crowned the summit of a green hill, where nothing more dangerous than a pouring rain could be expected to disturb its peace and safety.

When the first term in the new and most desirable quarters commenced, it was with a stranger as the teacher. Our little schoolmistress was to spend the winter in the home where she had been so tenderly cared for during the long time of bodily prostration which followed the overstraining of her nervous system at the time of her escape with the children under her care.

Busy with spinning-wheel and loom and sewing-machine, and with her diligent efforts to prepare Nils to enter with honour a higher school than that over which she had presided, the winter passed pleasantly away. Nils's examination surpassed the utmost expectations of his teacher. His sweet, grateful humility in the midst of honour was as touching as his humble submission to the great misfortune which had threatened to overshadow his whole life.

The little schoolmistress took, with the opening spring, the place of a private teacher—a position that she had been strongly urged to fill. Her first scholar was a tall fellow, who was sure he could learn from her in the higher branches much that was important for him to understand.

The second pupil, who came in later on, was a little chap. He did not understand Swedish, nor did he know much in any direction, it was said. But how could he expect a fair estimation of his abilities, when the judges were not at home in his language, nor he in theirs? He, however, improved rapidly, and was soon not only able to speak Swedish, but comprehended many matters so well that he was a great help to the younger pupils who came in by degrees to be taught. He was too, in a way, a teacher for the schoolmistress herself, and had his credentials from the very highest authority.

The class increased as years went on, and was ever a

delightful source of interest to the happy instructress. The children did not call her "teacher," or "mistress," or even "Miss Tora;" they said simply "mother," which she thought the sweetest name in the world.

As to the first, the tall scholar, who was what Nils had promised to be, her permanent pupil, he was not always as obedient and submissive as he might have been. Even when he sat opposite to her at the dinner-table, in the presence of stranger guests, he would sometimes, contrary to her express command, tell the story of the great April thaw, and the escape of the little schoolmistress with her pupils. Of course he was rebuked for his misdemeanour; but he only protested against her strict government, and declared that she could never get over "the schoolma'am." Yet he acknowledged she was always teaching him something worth knowing through what she was—the very best woman and the very best Christian he had ever had the pleasure of knowing.

This was, it must be confessed, an inexcusably obstreperous scholar; but Tora would not have exchanged her husband, her Gunner, the fast friend of her promising "brother Karl," for the meekest or the wisest man in the world.

A WEEK AT KULLEBY

CHAPTER I

CHURCH SERVICE

The church at Kulleby was no dear, old-fashioned Swedish church, with its low white stone walls and its high black roof. The bell had no quaintly-formed tower of its own outside and quite separate from the sacred edifice, like an ecclesiastical functionary whose own soul has never entered into the Holy of holies. No; the parish of Kulleby had its pride in a great new wooden sanctuary, with nothing about its exterior, from foundation to belfry, that might not be seen in any Protestant land whatever. Crowning the top of a green hill that rose in the midst of a wide stretch of rolling meadows stood the simple building. To it came on Sunday the rustics of the parish as regularly as they went to their week-day work. Only here and there in the unfenced churchyard rose a low mound to indicate where, as it were, a chance seed had been dropped into "God's acre."

It was Sunday morning. At eight o'clock the bell had sounded out over the green slopes, and even late sleepers were called to put on their best garments, whether church-goers or not church-goers, in honour of the holy day or holiday, as it might happen to be kept in their home. Then

came the second ringing, when prudent, far-away worshippers took psalm-book and pocket-handkerchief in hand and
started demurely, at a Sunday pace, for the house of God. At
a quarter to ten the clergyman had been seen in the dim
distance, and the fact was announced by "priest-ringing." At
ten came the "assembly-ringing," when talkers in the
churchyard must break off in the midst of a half-made
bargain, or check the but half-expressed sympathy with the
joy or sorrow of some fellow-rustic with whom there had
been a confidential chat.

Within, the church was all white, with here and there a
gilded line like a bright, holy purpose running through a
simple everyday life. There was a fresh, pure air about the
place, as if even angels might have gathered there in their
fair garments. The worshippers, however, on the women's
side were all in black—black dresses, and black kerchiefs
over the heads, like solemn, mourning penitents rather than
followers of the Psalmist who could say, "I was glad when
they said unto me, Let us go into the house of the Lord."
There were two exceptions to this sombre rule.

The seats facing each other on opposite sides of the chancel
were unoccupied, save by a tall young woman and a little
girl, who now hurriedly took their places, and in a formal,
perfunctory manner put down their heads for a supposed
private prayer for a blessing on this opportunity of public
worship. They very soon rose up mechanically, and looked
about them with the curious eyes of strangers.

The little girl, nipped, and it seemed almost blasted, by gales
of prosperity, showed a fair, round face, full and soft, and
satisfied with its worldly portion. The mouth, although it
looked as if it had tasted the good things of life, was sweet
and loving. Her companion was tall and strongly built, and
somewhat gaily dressed in garments made in every particular

according to the latest fashion. Two long ostrich feathers lazily lolled on the broad brim of her hat, as much at home as if they had never known any other abode; and her new kid gloves fitted her large hands to perfection—a fact of which it was plain she was conscious.

The clergyman was coming in, with the long black folds which were his authorized substitute for a gown hanging from the nape of his neck to the floor. In one hand he carried in full sight a white handkerchief, held in one corner like a drooping banner of peace.

There was suddenly a counter object of attention for the gay worshippers in the side pew. A little woman in black came hurrying up the aisle and entered the seat before them. She put down on the narrow shelf her prayer-book and a tumbled red handkerchief, and then bowed her head. Suddenly, in the midst of her devotions, she hastily withdrew the offending radical handkerchief, and substituted in its place a heavy linen one, so closely pressed, as if by mangling, that it lay by the psalm-book as uncompromisingly stiff as itself.

A smile passed over the features of the little girl, and she looked up into the face of her companion for sympathy. Instead of the responsive glance she expected, she saw an expression of pain which she was puzzled to understand.

The service went on. The sermon was long and tiresome, to judge from the impulsive movement of relief on the part of the little girl when all was at last over. She was well satisfied when her companion went down the aisle at an unusually rapid pace. The rustics generally lingered to hear when there was to be an auction, what letters were to be distributed, and other announcements by which a scattered congregation, rarely meeting through the week, might be made aware of matters secular and parochial which it was important for them to know.

The butterfly worshippers had, as it were, flown away when the mass of the congregation streamed out from the door. Long, narrow black lines stretched off in every direction as over the well-trodden paths the cottagers plodded away to their homes after this the periodical great event, recreation, and social gathering of their hard-working lives.

Alone the little woman in black took her way. Her goal was on the long rocky ridge that bounded the eastern horizon like a transplanted bit of the Jura. There was no path for her to follow, but she made her way over the meadows with the sure instinct of the swallow winging its flight to its winter home. He who careth for the birds would surely care for her. It was plain she was one of the humble of the earth in every sense of the word. Her black head kerchief was old and worn, and her clumsily-fitting, coarse cloth "sacque" stood out below her waist as if it were of sheet iron, while her spare skirts fell below it like a drooping flower-bell from its open calyx above. She was not thinking of her clothes. Her heart was warbling a song of thanksgiving.

CHAPTER II

AT THE PASTOR'S

Monday morning had come, with work for the workers and pleasure for the pleasure-seekers. The curate at Kulleby was one of the workers, and yet Monday, instead of Sunday, was really his day of rest. His last sermon having been delivered, fairly given over to his hearers to be digested, the new one was not to be begun before Tuesday. There must be one day in the week in which to draw a free breath before the real labour of his life was to be recommenced. The introduction to the discourse once mastered, as the first link, he added day by day to the lengthening chain—a perpetual wearying weight to him, and, it might be supposed, to become so for his hearers.

This would be a mistake. Had the curate preached in Hebrew or Greek, the reverent faces would have been respectfully turned towards him, with the honest conviction that somehow or other the listeners were undergoing a helpful and uplifting process through what the curate was pleased to say to them. He was reverenced and beloved, as he well deserved to be, and was to his people the bearer of good tidings—the messenger of peace. *He* was the message to them, through what he was and what he was striving to be, and not through those painfully-produced sermons.

Now for the morning he had dropped the pastor, and was simply the family father.

The humble home of the curate was separated from the public road by a great grass plot, through which a wide walk went straight, without a curve or a compromise, from the gate to the foot of the high wooden steps that led to the ever-open door.

The Saturday evening rake-marks were on the loose sand of the path, for the family had on Sunday, though in their holiday garments, used the side gate that led to the entrance at the back of the house. The garden was large and well cared for. Now the weekly weeding was going on, the father sitting like a general at a distance from the battle, but in constant communication with the soldiers in full fight in the cause of order, fruitfulness, and prosperity. The four small boys who were working so busily were not under strict military discipline, for free conversation was allowed so long as the hands continued as busy as the tongues.

The curate sat on a roughly-made but comfortable garden sofa, and was knitting on a strong stocking in sweet composure. A gay-coloured parallelogram stared out from the grass beside him; for there, covered with a patchwork quilt, lay, in a great basket, the baby, the little girl, the pride of the household, fast asleep. So the curate could not be said to be exactly idle, though he was taking a delicious morning rest. His wife meanwhile—a large-hearted, practical woman— was making all things comfortable in the house, with the help of her efficient *aide-de-camp*, an orphan girl snatched from the influences of the poorhouse. Where a specially strong arm was required, the curate himself was at all times to be relied upon. He was not only a hewer of wood, but often a bearer of wood as well as of water. He was, too, an embodied guild of all mechanical trades, and might have been warranted to use skilfully at a pinch any tools whatever.

The curate gave a start as the click of the front gate was heard, and almost impatiently wondered who could be coming.

A tall young woman walked rapidly along the rake-marked walk, and dotted it at regular intervals with the distinct portrait of the soles of her strong and well-made boots.

She went up the steps decidedly, and entered the house without knocking, as any ordinary visitor might have done. In a moment more she appeared in the garden, with the curate's wife at her side. He stood up and bowed awkwardly, and then looked inquiringly at the new-comer. He recognized at once in her the stranger who had sat near the chancel the day before, though her dress was somewhat different from her Sunday attire. She wore a black sailor hat, from which she had that morning removed the uplifted wings that threatened to take the whole head-gear upward, and had left only the broad, bright band that wound round it. She wore a short, dark travelling dress that well displayed her new boots. The visitor did not wait for the curate to speak, but said quickly, "I will only detain you a moment. Can you tell me where widow Marget Erikson lives, the old woman who sat in front, on the side benches, in the church yesterday?"

"Marget Erikson? Her I know very well, but it is not so easy to tell where she lives," answered the curate, with at the same time an inquiring glance at the stranger. A look of intelligence came into his face, and he said: "It is not—it cannot be! no," and he turned to the group of small boys, now all standing, some of them weeds in hand, wonderingly regarding the stranger. "Here, Kael," said the father, singling out a fair-haired, intelligent-looking little fellow, "you can show the young lady the way to widow Marget Erikson's." Again there was a scrutinizing, questioning look on the part of the pastor.

A slight flush tinged the cheek of the stranger. She was turning away with her guide, when the boy said hastily, "Where's the basket, mamma?"

"There'll be no basket to-day," she answered, almost with a smile. "You can take Marget this instead from me," and she picked from her favourite bush a large, half-open rosebud, with a long stem and rich, shining leaves.

The boy could hardly understand the love-prompted courtesy that would not send to the widow what might to a stranger seem like alms, but which really was but the sharing of what one poor Christian had with a poorer.

The guide trotted off with his bare feet across the meadow, where a little path showed that he was not the first to find a direct way from the parsonage to the widow's cottage.

"Well, wife? well, Anna?" said the pastor, and looked inquiringly into the face of his best-beloved, as he generally did when he was in doubt or difficulty. It was a face that any one might have been pleased to look upon. It had in it the bright cheeriness of a child, and at the same time dignity and a wisdom in this world's matters, as well as "the wisdom that cometh from above." He received no answer, and so said himself: "She was in church yesterday when you were at little Fia's death-bed. I could hardly help thinking of you and the child when I was in the midst of my sermon. The miller told me afterwards that 'miss' and the little girl were with Possessionaten something, a traveller who had stopped at the inn by the cross-road."

There was a sudden end put to the conversation by a loud cry from the baby, which swept all other expressions from the face of the pastor's wife, where at once mother love was triumphant.

CHAPTER III

A STRANGE MEETING

Across meadows, over ditches, and at last up rather a steep ascent wound the way to Widow Erikson's cottage. The path had grown rough and narrow, but the barefooted boy went over it as lightly and as unharmed as if he had been a happy bird. The boots, however, of his companion seemed a tight fit for climbing, and at last a straggling bramble that crossed the way turned up two little black points, like doors, to show the way to the untanned leather behind the bright polish. The traveller stopped, and smoothed them down in vain with her finger; the mischief was done. "This is an ugly, disagreeable path," she exclaimed, "and a long one too."

"Maybe," said the boy; "but summer and winter Widow Erikson comes down here all alone. I don't believe she'd miss the service if you'd give her a bucket of red apples." The boy had evidently named his ultimatum in the way of temptation. "There's the cottage," he added, pointing to a small, reddish-brown building far up the ascent.

"Give me the flower," said the stranger; "I will tell her who sent it. You go back now. You've shown me the way; I don't need you any longer. Thanks! Thank your mother too. Here!" and she laid in the boy's hand a bit of silver that made his face shine. He bowed in his best style, which did not disturb his backbone, but brought his chin down till it touched his breast. He had taken off his cap for the performance, and his white hair fluttered in the breeze as he watched his late companion making her way up to the cottage alone. All was right, he was sure, and down he ran as fast as his feet could carry him. The precious silver was stored in the depths of his pocket, and with it he bought in imagination all sorts of treasures before he reached home to tell the success of his errand.

The traveller moved slowly as the path grew more steep, and finally walked doubtfully on as she approached the cottage. There were three or four low steps leading to the door, and there some kind of an animal seemed making a vain attempt to go up. As the stranger drew nearer she saw that a small woman with a short, dark skirt was bowed over, evidently washing the steps, with her back towards the path and her unexpected guest. A noise near her made the figure stand upright and turn its face towards the new-comer. One sight of the visitor prompted a series of bobbing courtesies, a wondering look in the old sun-browned face, and a folding back into a triangular form of the wet sackcloth apron, which was truly not in a presentable condition. The old woman was the first to speak. "Good-day, miss—good-day!" and then there was a look of astonished inquiry.

"The pastor's wife sent you this," said the girl, holding out the beautiful rosebud she had taken from the boy.

"So like her!" said the old woman, lovingly. "She's just like that herself! God bless her! Thank her for me, please—thank her for me!" and the thin, work-distorted, wrinkled hand was hastily wiped on the apron, and then stretched out to take that of the stranger for the usual expression of gratitude. "Thank *you*, miss, for bringing it," continued the old woman, with another questioning look at her guest. "Do you know her—do you know the curate's wife? It's likely you don't live hereabouts." The cut of the stranger's clothes was not in vogue at Kulleby.

"Don't you know me?" said the young woman, in a low voice.

"No, miss!" was the answer, with another courtesy.

"Don't you know me, mother?" was the question that followed, while the fair face flushed with the effort those words had cost the speaker.

"It can't be my Karin!" was the exclamation. There was another period of courtesying, and a long look of almost unbelieving surprise. There was no move to take this changed daughter by the hand, nor was there any such action on the part of the girl.

"I was stopping at the inn with Possessionaten Bilberg and his little daughter, the one I have taken care of so long. I found out you were in this neighbourhood, and so I got some one to show me the way to where you were living." She did not say that she had seen her mother at church, nor would she have liked to own, even to herself, that she was now repulsed by the appearance and manners of one to whom she was bound by the strongest of ties.

"Come in," said the old woman, courtesying as to a stranger. "It's a poor place, but you are welcome."

A poor place it was indeed, and Karin with her belongings looked there like a transplanted flower from a far country. They who had once been so near to each other seemed now to have almost no common ground on which to meet.

"I did not know how you had it, mother," said Karin at last. She had been silenced by her first view of the poor room.

"It is worse than it was in Norrland, when you went away, so long ago. Your brother Erik came home, and was wild-like, as he always was. He pulled himself down, and was sick a long while, and then he died. There was the funeral, and the doctor, and all that; and there was not much left, for of course I couldn't do a turn of work while I was nursing him."

"Just like him, to take all you had!" said the daughter, indignant.

The old woman did not seem to notice the angry exclamation. A sudden light made beautiful the old face as she said: "He came round at the last, and almost like an angel. It did me good to hear him talk. I didn't mind anything when he had come round. I am sure he went to heaven when he died. He was my only boy, and I loved him!" she continued, as if she were speaking to a stranger; and then suddenly remembering who her visitor was, she added: "You would not have known him for the same. 'Tell Karin,' he said to me—'tell her she must forgive me. Tell her to remember she'll need to have her sins forgiven some time. There's only one way.' He said so!" and there was another courtesy of apology that she was talking so to that strange young lady who said she was her daughter.

"Oh dear!" said Karin, looking at her watch, "I must go now. Possessionaten and his little girl were out for a drive, and I did not leave any word at the inn where I was going. I will come soon again. Don't feel hard to me about Erik or anything. Remember I did not know how you had it. They wrote me there was a cottage somewhere you could live in free, and I thought you were getting on pretty well."

"Yes, I have the cottage free. The curate's wife comes from the north. He married up there, and they came to visit her folks. She heard about me, for she was there when Erik died. She knew about this cottage, and nothing would do but I must come down with them; and so I did. You can't think how kind they have been to me. I've done a power of knitting since I have been here. She sees that somebody buys my stockings. But you must go. Come again," said the old woman, in strange confusion between her daughter that was ten years ago and this strange young lady who had condescended to look in upon her.

They parted without even a shake of the hand. The old woman stood at the door and watched the tall girl hurrying down the path, and felt almost as if she had been in a troubled dream.

CHAPTER IV

TOO LATE

Possessionaten Bilberg was subject to transient indisposi-
tions on Sunday morning. The symptoms that had prevented
his being at the church service the day before seemed to have
disappeared entirely on Monday. He came home from his
drive with his daughter in unusually good spirits; and as for
little Elsa, she was quite delighted. She had had a nice play
with some charming children, and there was a baby in the
house, which she had really been allowed to carry in her own
willing arms. Karin's overshadowed countenance passed
unnoticed in the general stir that followed the return of the
father and daughter. They had been invited to spend several
days at the hospitable country home where they had been so
warmly welcomed. It had been urged that while Elsa was
happy with playmates of her own age, Possessionaten could
see many things in the neighbourhood that might be
suggestive to him, interested as he was in agriculture and
manufactures. Planning and packing took all the afternoon,
and towards evening the carriage was at the door, and Elsa
and her father were to take their departure.

"I was afraid you would be lonely, Karin, and sorry we are
going away; but you don't seem to mind it at all," said the
little girl, in an injured tone.

"So you want me to be sorrowful," answered Karin, trying to be playful.

"No, no! but I thought you would miss me, and I was glad when papa said you could keep on sleeping in my nice room, and be as comfortable as anybody."

There was a little condescension in the tone, though it was affectionate; but Karin did not notice it, for she was accustomed to Elsa's airs and graces. Karin really drew a sigh of relief when the carriage drove away and she was left to herself. It was not a pleasant evening that she spent, filled with the thronging reminiscences of the past and a full realization of her own shortcomings. To-morrow she would make another visit to her mother, and try to be more frank and affectionate.

The morning came, and Karin was busy clearing all traces of a traveller's comfort from the capacious bag that Elsa had been allowed to give her for the journey. It really would hold a great deal, and filled it was to the uttermost at the country shop to which Karin easily found her way; tea, sugar, and tempting articles of diet, which she hoped her mother would enjoy. It was heavy, but Karin rather liked to feel the pain in her arm, from bearing her unusual burden. She easily found her way along the upward path, and exhilarated by the exercise and the pleasure she was about to give, she entered the cottage in a very cheerful frame of mind. All was silent within.

In the box sofa-bed of the single room there was some one lying, pale and still. "She is dead!" was the first wild thought of distress; but a sweet, broken voice murmured something about Erik and heaven. It was plain that the old woman was wandering in mind, and lost in visions of the past.

Karin unpacked her basket in a hurry. There were the preparations of the night before for the fire and the boiling of the water for the morning meal, to be simple indeed. Yet there was a packed basket, "the basket" no doubt from the parsonage. She did not unpack it, though it seemed filled with food. She made some tea in haste, and took it with a biscuit to her mother's side. She put the cup on a chair near her, and sitting down on the edge of the bed, she lifted up the old woman, passing one strong arm about the little body. There was gentleness and kindness in the touch. The old head was voluntarily drooped caressingly against the breast of her daughter; there was a long sigh, and Karin knew she was motherless. Repentant, sorrowing tears flowed fast. There was no opportunity left for reparation in this world. That loving last movement towards her was the only pleasant thought on which Karin could dwell.

How still it was in the cottage! The birches without scarcely quivered in the soft summer air, and not even the twitter of a bird was to be heard.

Karin had just gently laid the old head on the pillow, when a form, almost to her as of an angel, suddenly appeared at the door. It was the pastor's wife, her face beaming with the tender interest she was feeling for the lone dweller in the cottage. She understood the whole as she saw Karin's streaming tears, and the changed old face beside her.

"My mother is dead!" said Karin simply, but in a broken voice.

"I am glad she saw her good daughter before she died," said the pastor's wife comfortingly.

"I am no good daughter!" exclaimed Karin bitterly. It was a relief to confess her selfishness, her forgetfulness of her mother, in the midst of her own comfortable surroundings, and her cold willingness to believe that all was well with that old woman, who she had supposed was still in the far north.

The pastor's wife listened in silence. She had no words of comfort to say. Here was a case beyond her treatment. She did not kneel, but she clasped her hands and sat quite still, while she laid Karin's sorrow and penitence before the dear Lord Jesus, so ready to forgive, and to heal the broken, repentant heart. When she had closed the prayer with a fervent "Amen!" which seemed to be the sealing of her petitions to the One strong to save, she turned to Karin and said, "I will go down and send a person to watch her, and then you must go with me to our home; for I have heard that you were left at the inn. You cannot be there now." She felt that it would be best for Karin to be for a time alone. She had brought her to the heavenly Presence, and she left her there to commune with the pitiful Father in heaven.

CHAPTER V

KARIN AND ELSA

There was a new, low mound in the churchyard. Kind young hands from the curate's had covered it with evergreen boughs, and sprinkled among them bright flowers, so that it seemed but a slight swell in the green sweep around it dotted with daisies.

Karin had begun a new phase in her life. She had something to love and respect which had no taint of this present world and the worldliness reigning therein. She had entered humbly and heartily into the simple life at the curate's home, where she had been so lovingly welcomed.

That thin man, with the angular, loosely-built figure, with a speaking expression of poverty about it; that man whose shabby Sunday coat had not a button-hole that did not publicly tell of privately-done repairs by his wife's untailor-like hand; that man whose very hair was scanty, and was changing colour—she looked up to him as if he had been a prince. And so he was; for he had a Father who was King over all the nations of the earth, who loved him as a son, and received from that son the happy, truthful affection of a true child.

Mrs. Woods Baker

That woman who went about in the simplest of garments, and shunned no form of labour that made the home more comfortable or attractive, had become to Karin a model of all that was pure and lovely and lovable. The baby, who fell much to her care, seemed to have a healing influence on her wounded, humbled, penitent heart. It had for her its artless smile, and its little arms went out to her as trustfully as if she had never strayed from the narrow path. Karin had a new standard in life, a new picture of what she wished to be, a new way of estimating her fellow-creatures.

Karin was glad that circumstances made it necessary for her to lay down in the depths of her capacious trunk the gay garments that had been her pride. There had been no dressmaking, no consulting of milliner or *modiste*. Like most Swedish girls, she had a black dress; she had but to put a crape band over her sailor-hat, and let the short crape veil fall over her solemnized face, and her mourning suit was for the present complete.

This time, this precious time, went away all too rapidly, but it swept from Karin the impressions of years, and strengthened in her, day by day, the new purposes and the new hopes that had sprung up in the midst of her humiliation and distress.

From the cottage in the woods the daughter had but taken away her mother's "psalm-book" in its close-fitting black cotton case, her worn Bible, and the carefully-folded white handkerchief that lay under them. In the corner of the handkerchief a large K had been embroidered by unskilful hands. Karin knew it as one of her own early trophies, that had been given to her mother in pride when she had received it as a reward for skill shown in the sewing-class at school. This little remembrance of her had been treasured and prized while she was living in selfish forgetfulness of the poor old woman far away. Repentant tears had fallen on the humble memento.

On the morning of the day when Possessionaten Bilberg and his daughter were expected, the curate's wife went with Karin to the inn.

The parting between them was full of grateful expression on the one side, and of tender interest and kind advice on the other. They were never to meet again on earth, but they had a common Father in heaven above, in whose presence they trusted one day to be united.

Karin was, of course, on the steps of the inn to receive her charge. It was not unusual for Karin to wear sometimes a black dress, and Elsa, in her pleasure at the meeting and her eagerness to tell her late experiences, did not notice anything particularly serious in the face of the maid. When, however, they were alone together, she looked up suddenly, and saw that Karin's eyes were full of tears as she was struggling to speak of what had befallen her.

"What is it? what is the matter?" asked Elsa affrightedly.

"My mother is dead! I have lost my mother!" said Karin simply.

Elsa cast her arms around Karin's neck in an unusual fit of demonstrative affection, and wept with her. "O Karin, what will you do? How you must have loved her! How sorry you must be! I have thought a great deal about a mother since I have been away. I have always missed something, and felt that I was different from other little girls, but I did not really understand what it was. I have had everything I wanted, and papa has been so kind, and you too, Karin, but there was something. Where I have been the children did so love their mamma, and she made it so charming for them, and she had such a sweet way with them;" and here the little girl sobbed, more, it must be owned, from thinking of what she had missed in her life than from sympathy for Karin, and yet they were drawn nearer together than ever before.

The stir of the arrival of Possessionaten Bilberg and his daughter had passed away from about the inn, and stillness reigned around on every side, on the wide meadows in front, and on the long, low, rocky ridge beyond them. Possessionaten Bilberg was smoking a cigar in the wide porch, and quietly thinking. Elsa had flown down to tell him of Karin's trouble, and now he greeted the trusted maid almost with respect as she came to him to ask some questions about their approaching departure.

He got up stiffly and took Karin by the hand, as he said simply, "I am sorry to hear that you have had trouble. Your mother was old, I daresay," he added, as he dropped her hand.

"Yes, old and feeble," was the reply.

Karin waited a moment, and then began to speak of the journey.

"Yes; it will be this evening," he said, and his face wore a most peculiar expression, as if some struggle was going on within him.

At last he began: "I have had time to see more of Elsa than usual, and when she was with young companions. There is something about her as if her pleasure were the most important thing to everybody, and she rather thought nobody was quite equal to herself."

It is possible that these peculiarities had become Elsa's by inheritance, as her father was not without his own tendencies in that direction—a fact of which he was naturally unconscious.

He went on: "You have been a good girl, Karin, and I am pleased with you. Elsa needs now some one who has a right to take her more steadily in hand."

There was a pause, and the tears sprang to Karin's eyes. Was she to be dismissed, when she felt almost as much at home in her master's house as his daughter herself?

"Yes, you have been a good girl, Karin, and you deserve your reward. You never ought to leave my home. What Elsa needs, though, is a mother's care. She needs one who with a mother's name will have a strong right to her respect and her affection."

He paused a moment. Karin, not knowing what else to do, dropped a courtesy, and waited for him to go on. He got up, blushed, took a few steps on the piazza, and then turned and said abruptly: "I am going to be married, and I want you to tell Elsa about it. Tell her that it is the lady whom the children called 'aunty' there in the country—their mother's sister. She is willing to marry me. I never thought to get such a good wife." And Possessionaten Bilberg looked humble, for perhaps the first time in his life.

"She is not like me in many things," he continued, as if pleased with his subject. "She is pious—something I don't quite understand, but it makes me sure she will be a good mother to Elsa. I really believe she would hardly have taken me if she had not longed to get my child under her care," said Possessionaten, with another unwonted attack of humility. "Please tell Elsa at once," he said, and sat down again, to indicate that the interview was over.

In a few moments Elsa came flying along the piazza, and surprised her father by taking a seat on his knee and putting her arms round his neck. "Papa! papa!" she said, "how could you think of doing anything that would please me so much?"

"Your own mother loved her, Elsa, and so I am sure she is the right kind of a woman, and that you will be happy together."

Possessionaten had spoken in a matter-of-fact sort of way, and Elsa went upstairs in a less ecstatic mood than when she came down, and told Karin calmly that her father seemed pleased that she liked having a new mother.

CHAPTER VI

CHRISTMAS EVE

Christmas Eve had come. There had been joy in the curate's home—carols and prayer around the lighted tree, the distribution of simple gifts, and the consumption of any amount of rice porridge. Even the grave pastor had grown playful as the evening went on. This had prompted one of the boys to exclaim that he was the very best father in the world—a comprehensive assertion that was approved by all parties present. The power to cast off care and even serious thought for a time, and frolic with children, was one of the secrets of the curate's personal power. In his sacred capacity he was above and apart from all; as a father or a friend he was near and familiarly dear to all, even to the youngest in his household and the humblest of his people.

Now he gave a start, and there was a look of astonishment all round the family as there was the sound of heavy cart-wheels grinding along over the sand under the parsonage windows.

In another moment there was a steady tramping on the side steps, then through the passage to the dining-room, where the family were assembled.

Four strong men were bearing a huge box, and now entered,

Mrs. Woods Baker

much embarrassed at being unable to take off their caps in the presence of the pastor, but their deep voices pronounced a "Good Yule!" and their thick, soft caps went off in a hurry when they had deposited their heavy burden. "We were to open it, pastor," they said, and they forthwith produced their tools from the slouching pockets of their strong coats. The pastor's wife disappeared instantly, thinking, as usual, of others more than of herself; for she, too, would have liked a peep into the box when the thick boards had been thrown up and the packed stores were first visible. She had, however, what pleased her better—some hot coffee, a cake of saffron bread, and the remains of the porridge on the table in the kitchen when the last nail had been drawn out. The men disappeared, grinning with satisfaction; while the wondering children superintended, with occasional wild dances and leaps of delight, the unfolding of the secrets of the wonderful box.

A prosperous "possessionat" who had learned that the chief joy of possession is the power of giving had sent household stores on a munificent scale. A happy wife, accustomed to see her own husband always dressed as for a holiday, having a full remembrance of the pastor's outer man, and of his wife's forgetfulness of herself, had sent for him a full black suit, and for his wife a handsome dark dress, as well as a warm fur cape. A little girl, who had learned to remember that there were other people beside herself to be thought of in the world, had selected books and toys for the children. The orphan girl had not been forgotten. She looked with astonishment at the substantial winter coat that had been marked with her name, and wondered who could have thought of *her*. There was still a beautiful, closely-woven white basket, with a firm handle, at one side of the box. It was lifted out and opened. There were all sorts of things— potted, canned, dried, and preserved, to make, with good bread and butter, a nice evening meal for an unexpected guest; a most welcome present in a family where hospitality never failed, and yet the larder was often scantily provided. At the bottom of the basket lay a card, on which was written, "From a humble friend, in remembrance of 'the basket.'"

The tears rushed to the eyes of the curate and his wife, and their hands met, while their thoughts were with the little old cottage saint now in heaven, and a prayer was sent up for the daughter that she might continue to walk in the ways of peace.

"O mamma, what a good basket to keep all your mending in!" said one of the boys.

"Just what I will do," said the mother; "I shall like to have it always near me."

"Do put on your new suit, papa," urged the children. He vanished into his room close at hand, and soon reappeared transformed into a new and complete edition of his old self, as it were, in a fine fresh binding.

The suit was not a perfect fit, but hung less loosely about him than his wonted best garments, made long, long ago.

The pastor playfully walked up and down the room with a consequential air, to the great amusement of the children. "You will wear your new suit to-morrow!" they exclaimed, one after another, as in the refrain of a song.

"On New-Year's Day, perhaps," said the father. "For to-morrow I like my old suit best; for we are to remember then how the loving Lord of all humbled Himself to be the Babe of Bethlehem."

There were a few words of prayer and thanksgiving, and then

66 Mrs. Woods Baker

the family, with a kiss all round, parted for the night.

Perchance the angels who sang again the Christmas song, "On earth peace, good will toward men," lingered over the curate's home with a kindred feeling for him; for was he not, too, a messenger, sent "to minister for them who shall be heirs of salvation"?

ALF

CHAPTER I

A FOOLISH RESOLVE

Tall, handsome, and young; that one saw at a single glance. The age of the lad it was not easy to determine. The mind wavered between sixteen and nineteen, but sixteen it really was. It was no true Swedish face, yet such faces are often found among the fair children of the North. The boy had a clear, dark complexion, and his waving hair was intensely black. His nose was decided, but there was a weakness about the small mouth that seemed quite inconsistent with the fiery glance of the full brown eyes.

It was late, yet he was sitting looking steadily before him, while his thoughts were evidently wandering. "*So* they want me to promise, and *so* they want me to live?" he said at last. "I cannot make promises I do not mean to keep. I can do many things, but I cannot take a false position as to what I intend to be." He stood up and straightened his whole person with an admiring self-respect as he spoke.

He would not be compelled by public opinion to do that for which he was not inclined! He was old enough to choose for himself, and choose he would! He would not be confirmed!

Mrs. Woods Baker

He would not assume obligations contrary to his wishes, and make professions he did not honestly mean! There seemed to him to be in this something noble, something determined, something manly, and he pleasantly reflected upon his righteous independence.

The confirmation was appointed for the morrow. He had seen the slender, swift horse that was to be his—a gift from his father. He knew a gold watch was lying in his mother's drawer, to be one of his many presents to commemorate the important occasion. The guests were invited for the splendid dinner his parents were to give in his honour. He would be expected to appear in one of the stylish new suits provided for him as now a fully-grown young gentleman. He would be toasted, complimented, and, in short, the hero of the day in that beautiful home. He knew that his mother had retired early. She was doubtless praying for him then, and would be on the morrow. She, at least, would expect him to keep his promises. She should know that he would not disgrace her by a false oath.

His pocket-book was well filled by a munificent present from his grand-uncle in America. He could go where he pleased. He took out a small, light trunk from one of his closets, and it was soon packed with his new garments and a few specially dear personal valuables. There were no books but the pocket Bible, in which his mother had so lately written his name. For her sake he would take it with him, and for her sake he would open it at least for five minutes every day.

Stealthily he crept down the staircase and through the broad halls, dropped from a low window, and was soon in the open air. There was a light still in the stable-boy's room, and he would so have help for the harnessing of the horse, and an opportunity to leave a parting message for his mother.

He moved slowly and silently. He looked in through the small panes, and could see the boy bending over a book. He tapped gently. There was a start, and the door was opened in a moment.

"I am going to town, Lars," he said, "and I want your help. Get up the spring wagon as soon as you can."

The stable-boy looked suspiciously at his young master, and at the small trunk he had set down beside him. "Where is Master Alf going?" asked the boy anxiously. "Anything dreadful happened? Won't you be here for the confirmation?"

"No; it's that that sends me away," was the answer. "I can't even seem to make promises I don't intend to keep. I mean to be an honourable gentleman, and I shall not begin that way. Come, hurry!"

"But stop, Master Alf! Why don't you make the promises and try to keep them?" said the stable-boy.

"I suppose that is what you mean to do—eh?" said the young gentleman scornfully.

"It would be my duty any way to live right," was the answer. "I can't see that the promises make any difference. I ought to live right, I know, and I mean to try. It won't be easy. That's all I understand about it." The round, dull face of the boy expressed clear determination, and he looked his young master full in the eyes as he spoke. "Perhaps you've made up your mind to go wrong!" he added, with a doubtful look at his companion.

"Do as I bid you, and get up the horse at once!" said Alf, in a commanding tone. "Tell my mother what I have said to you, and tell her, too, I have taken with me the Bible she gave me, and I'll read in it a bit every day for her sake. *I* believe in keeping promises. As for you, you'll find the team at the usual stable; you must go in early to-morrow for it."

"Where are you going, Master Alf?" urged the boy. "I'm afraid it's clean out to the bad!"

"That's none of your business! You don't know how a gentleman feels about a promise," was the answer.

"My father is here for the confirmation. He talked to me about that matter last night," persisted Lars. "He said when people were married they promised they would be good to each other, but that was their duty any way, if they were man and wife, promise or no promise. About confirmation, he said that was a good old custom that it was well to follow, but any way when boys get to our age they've got to make up their minds what sort of men they mean to be, and start clear and determined on the right track, or else they'll be sure, as the world is, to go to the bad. He said, too, we'd better be in a hurry, and have that fixed, for there was no saying how long even young folks would live. Young folks might be broken off right sudden, like a green branch in a high wind. I do wish you, Master Alf, could hear my father talk about this thing."

"I've heard you talk; that's quite enough of the family for me!" said Alf impatiently. "Attend to your business at once, will you, or I shall have to harness the horse myself."

"I *wish* my father was here, I do!" murmured Lars to himself, as he most unwillingly obeyed.

"That's for your sermon," said Alf, as he took the reins in his hand, and tossed a bit of silver to the serious, stolid-faced boy who was looking so sorrowfully at him.

As Alf said his last words to Lars, he wished in his heart that he had the stable-boy's full, simple determination to do right whatever it might cost him. The veil of self-contentment had fallen from Alf's eyes. His motives for what he was now doing stood out plainly before him. It was true that he did not wish to pledge himself openly to a life he did not intend to lead, but it was also true that it had long been his cherished wish to be free from the restraints of home, and able to yield to any and all the temptations that assailed him. He was voluntarily giving himself up to an evil, reckless life, and he knew it.

Mrs. Woods Baker

CHAPTER II

AFTER THIRTY YEARS

The slender birches were sunning their mottled stems in the warm spring air; the evergreen woods rose dark and mysterious; while the glad little spruces that skirted the thickets were nourishing soft buds on every twig, little caring that they would in time be as gloomy and solemn as the grand old veterans of the forest behind them.

Sweden once more! All seemed unchanged after thirty years, save the emigrant and whatever specially concerned him. The familiar homes far back from the road, he remembered them well. His own home, he knew, had been ravaged by fire, and scarcely a vestige of it remained. His parents were no more. He could not, if he had wished it, shed penitent tears over their graves; for their bones were mouldering in a far-away ancestral vault, with no kindly grass to mantle them, and no glad wild flowers to whisper of a coming resurrection. The possessions that should have been his had been willed away to strangers. The once well-known family name was now rarely heard in the neighbourhood, and then only sorrowfully whispered as connected with the sad and almost forgotten past.

It was Sunday morning. The church bell had rung out its

peals the appointed number of times, and now all was silent, for the rustic worshippers were gathered within the sacred walls.

The congregation were all seated, and the Confession was being repeated, when a tall, slender man, with peculiarly broad shoulders and a peculiarly small waist, came with an ungainly gait up the aisle, holding in his hand a limp felt hat as if it were glued fast to his long, thin fingers.

He stopped a moment, as if mechanically, before a full pew, and then stood doubtfully in the aisle.

A little chubby girl perched just behind him had not been too devout to observe the proceedings of the stranger. She unhooked the door of the seat in which she was established alone with her mother. The slight click attracted, as she had hoped, the attention of the new worshipper. She whispered to her bowed mother, "He has no place to sit; may I let him in to us?" The head was slightly nodded in reply; the door was gently pushed open; and the stranger sat down in the offered place. His dark face was thin, and wrinkled too much apparently for his years. His thick black hair and beard were irregularly streaked in locks with white, rather than grey with the usual even sprinkling brought about by age alone; and his forehead threatened to stretch backward far beyond the usual frontal bounds. He apparently took no part in the service. His eyes seemed looking far away from priest and altar, and his ears were dead to the words that fell upon them.

Above the chancel there had been a painting representing the Lord's Supper, not copied even second or third hand from Leonardo's masterpiece, but from the work of some far more humble artist. The cracks that had crept across the cloth of the holy table and scarred the faces of the disciples were no longer to be seen. The disciples, whose identity had so occupied the minds of the little church-goers and been the subject of week-day discussions, were now hidden with the whole scene from the eyes of all beholders. A red curtain veiled the long-valued painting in its disfigured old age. Against this glowing background was suspended a huge golden cross of the simplest construction. It was, in fact, the work of the carpenter of the neighbourhood, and was gilded by the hand of the pastor's wife, who had solemnly thought to herself as she wielded the brush, "We must look to the cross before we may draw near to the holy supper."

Some idea like this flitted through the mind of the stranger, though he did not appear like a devout worshipper. His whole bearing gave quite another impression. Even when, during prayers later on, he held up his hat before his face, as is supposed to be a devout attitude in some Christian lands, the little girl fancied she could see him peeping here and there round the church, as if he were taking an inventory of its specialties. It was but a simple country church, with square pillars of masonry supporting the galleries, from whence light wooden columns rose to the vaulted roof. Indeed, in the old-fashioned building the rural seemed to have been the only style of architecture attempted. The whole interior had been thoroughly whitewashed, however it had fared with the hearts of the worshippers.

During the sermon the stranger was evidently lost in his own meditations. As soon as the service was over, he followed the clergyman down the aisle to the sacristy, on one side of the main door.

The reverend gentleman was in the midst of disrobing, when the dark-faced man hastily entered and said abruptly, "Will you kindly look over this paper, which must be my only credential with you? I belong to this parish, and should be glad to have the privileges of membership when broken down and needing a home."

The pastor glanced at the paper. It was a simple certificate, from a well-known dignitary high in authority in the land, requesting that the bearer, without being subject to further investigation, should have his right acknowledged as a member of the parish to which he now made application. The pastor could treat him accordingly, only showing the paper in case any difficulty arising from this arrangement should make such publicity necessary.

The paper was properly signed, witnessed, and sealed. The pastor put it in his pocket, looked wonderingly at the applicant, and said, "The poorhouse is but a mean place, with accommodation for a few persons, and the present occupants are of the humblest sort. There are now living there an old woman, formerly a servant in respectable families, who has a room to herself; a half-mad fellow, who will not speak when spoken to unless he can hit on some way of answering in rhyme. He, of course, has a room to himself. There is, besides, a large room with sleeping-places for two persons. One of these places is occupied by an old man who has been a hard drinker; you would have to share the room with him. Would you be contented with that arrangement?"

"Contented and grateful," said the stranger. His name was given as "A. Johanson," and was so registered in the pastor's note-book. Particular directions were then kindly lavished on the stranger as to how he was to reach his future home.

A peculiar smile stole over the face of the listener. He took politely the permit which ensured his admittance at the last refuge of the unfortunate, and then, with a bow and a slight waving of the limp hat, he disappeared.

Mrs. Woods Baker

CHAPTER III

IN THE POORHOUSE

The poorhouse was not an imposing structure, but it could boast of antiquity, as it had been built long, long ago for the purpose for which it was now used.

It was not difficult for Johanson to locate the poorhouse poet. His room, like the other two, opened directly on the vestibule. On his own door he had been allowed to paint his name and publish his chosen occupation:—

"I take my bag,
My legs my nag,
And never fail
To fetch the mail."

So ran the poor rhymes, yet the mad poet had not given himself his full meed of praise. No storm was too wild, no cold too severe, no snow too deep for the faithful mail-carrier to make his rounds. Rather than give up the leathern bag entrusted to him to teasing country boys or desperate highwayman, he would have died in its defence.

The principle of growth had exerted its power eccentrically with the poorhouse poet. His legs and neck were elongated out of all proportion to the rest of his body. His small, pale face was raised unnaturally high in the air, as if he had suffered decapitation and his head had been posted as an assurance that offended law had been avenged. Unconscious of his own peculiarities, the persistent rhymer went about pleased with himself and all the world. Now he was particularly happy, for he considered himself a kind of presiding officer at the poorhouse, and as such the proper person to show the premises to curious strangers, or to formally install new inmates. On the entrance of Johanson with the pastor's permit, the poet immediately took the odd-looking pauper in hand, to make him at home in the establishment.

He knocked at the small room opposite the main entrance, and a shrill voice having shouted, "Come in!" the visitors opened the door.

"I bring a new-comer,
Our guest for the summer!
He's Johanson, he;
Gull Hansdotter, she."

So presented, Johanson bowed to the little old woman, who stood up beside the chair in which she had been sitting, and deigned to bend her knees for a courtesy just sufficiently to bring her short skirts possibly one inch nearer the floor. Her stiff demeanour, however, changed suddenly as she darted to a corner and produced a bit of rag carpet, on which she requested the visitors to stand, as her room had been freshly scoured for Sunday.

"Scour Sunday,
Scour Monday,
Scour every day,
That's her way,"

Mrs. Woods Baker

said the poet, retiring precipitately with his companion. The poet had described the absorbing pursuit of his fellow-lodger. Chairs, table, and floor in that little room were subject to such rasping purifications, that if there had ever been paint on any of them, it was a thing of the far past, while an ashy whiteness and a general smell of dampness were the abiding peculiarities of the apartment. The eyes of the owner had become possessed of a microscopic power of discovering the minutest speck that might have been envied by any scientific observer of insect life.

The poet next threw open the door of the room opposite his own, as he said to his companion,—

"Here is your place—
No want of space;
According to diet,
Not always so quiet."

These were the quarters Johanson was to share with the broad-chested man in a big chair, who sat with a stout stick beside him, as if ready at any moment to meet the attack of a roving marauder.

"This is our cellar-master,
Who lived faster and faster,
Till here with us he had to be.—
It's Johanson who comes with me;
He'll share your room, at least to-night,
And longer if you treat him right."

There was only an inhospitable grunt from the gouty, red-faced man whose biography had been more justly than politely abridged for the new-comer.

Johanson had no luggage to deposit. He thanked his

conductor for the trouble he had taken, and then seated himself on a wooden chair on his side of the room, and had evidently no further need of his guide, who promptly disappeared.

Johanson seemed gazing out of the window, but was really seeing nothing, while quite lost in his own thoughts, and altogether forgetful of his companion.

There was a pounding on the floor, followed by a rumbling sound, as of some one preparing to speak, and then the other occupant of the room said roughly: "Here, you! Do you see that crack across the middle of the floor, with three big, dark knots in the middle on each side of it? That's my landmark. You come over it, and there'll be mischief!"

"I shall take great pleasure in attending to your wishes. It is not likely that I shall visit you often," said Johanson, rising and bowing with much politeness, and then promptly resuming his seat.

The next step of the new lodger was to take a small, carefully-covered book from his pocket. The gilt edges, dulled by time, were, however, observed by the watchful spectator, a prisoner in his chair. The fine print and the divided verses were evident to his keen eyes, that twinkled in their red frames with an uncanny light. "No hypocrisy here! it don't take. Put up that book, or I'll throw my friend here at you. I never miss, so look out!" He touched the club-like stick beside him.

Johanson quickly put his hand in his breast-pocket and took out a small revolver. "Here is *my* friend," he said. "I never miss with this in my hand!" He spoke coolly, but his eyes were fearless and determined. "You let me alone, and I'll let you alone. I want to live peaceably. I shall do what I please on my side of the room, and I want no meddling from you."

The cellar-master understood at once that he had here a person not to be trifled with, and from that day there was no difficulty between them.

The revolver may or may not have been loaded, but the sight of it had been enough for the cellar-master, as for many a "rough" before.

As to the little woman who had given Johanson so ungracious a reception on his first appearance in her room, he had evidently taken an aversion to her society. When she came into his duplicated quarters, he was always looking out into the street, or so occupied that she had a better view of his back than of his face. He never named her, nor was she ever mentioned in the establishment by her lawful cognomen, but was always spoken of as "she," representing alone, as she did, her own sex in the poorhouse.

It seemed to her a wonder that with all her claims to respectability she had ever found her way to her present home. The walls of her room were decorated with silhouettes of this or that grand personage in whose service she had enjoyed the honour of being in days of yore. Such mementoes failing her, there were coveted seals to letters, or paper headings cut out and duly pointed at the edges, to shine forth from red backgrounds. A daguerreotype of herself, in all the buxom freshness of youth and the "bravery" of a gaily-adorned peasant costume, was always to be seen standing on her bureau half open, like the book of an absent-minded scholar disturbed in his researches. Her pretensions imposed not a little upon the cellar-master, who treated her with a certain respect; but the poet was unmindful of her social claims, and perhaps took a pleasure in showing his independence of her rule. Rule it was, for she condescended to cook for "those poor men folks," as she called them.

Not that her cooking was ever of an elaborate order—coffee and porridge being the only dainties on which she was permitted to display her full powers. Warming up and making over other dishes kindly sent in by benevolent neighbours she did to perfection, and showed in this matter an ingenuity most remarkable. When, however, she took in the meals she had prepared for the various recipients, it was with a studied ungraciousness, abated only for the cellar-master, who, as she said, had a respectable title of his own, and was suitable company for her.

Johanson, who had come to his present abode empty-handed, provided himself by degrees with needful articles of clothing of the simplest sort, as well as necessities for the toilet and the writing-table. The pen was much in his hand. It was used occasionally for a letter to the nearest large city, and such a missive was generally followed by a parcel, which was stowed away at once in the capacious chest appointed for his use.

The cellar-master was sure that it was on sheets ruled like music-paper that Johanson was almost constantly writing, though they were locked up in his chest almost before they were fairly dry. He did not seem to be a reader, but the objectionable little book with the gilt edges came out at a regular hour each day, and for five minutes at least had his full attention, without offensive interruption.

On the whole, the poorhouse had become for Johanson a peaceful and in a measure a comfortable home.

Mrs. Woods Baker

CHAPTER IV

PREPARING FOR CONFIRMATION

With the autumn began for the pastor the most pleasing duty of the year—the instruction of his class for confirmation. He announced in church one Sunday that after the service he would be in the sacristy to take the names of any of the young people who wished to join the proposed class. He was sitting in the sacristy at the appointed time, with a group of young rustics standing about him, when Johanson came quietly in.

"I can attend to you first," said the pastor, turning kindly towards the dark-bearded man.

"I can wait; I am in no hurry," was the reply.

The waiting was long, as had been expected. When the boys and girls had all gone out, Johanson stepped to the pastor's side and said, "Please put down my name."

"For what?" asked the pastor, in astonishment.

"For the confirmation class," was the calm reply. "I have never been confirmed."

The pastor had noticed, naturally, that Johanson had not been forward to the Lord's Supper even when the cellar-master had been helped up the aisle from the poorhouse seat near the door, and Gull and the half-mad poet had decorously followed. At this he had hardly been surprised, for there were other members of the congregation who did not communicate more than once a year. The good man felt a sudden repulsion towards the stranger still without the Christian pale.

"You wish then to be confirmed?" said the pastor, looking Johanson directly in the eye.

"I wish to receive the instruction, and it will be your duty to judge of my fitness afterwards," was the reply.

"Perhaps I could find time to teach you privately, though it is a busy season, with all the certificates of removal and that kind of thing," said the pastor doubtfully.

"I would rather be taught as you teach these young people," said Johanson. "Please try to forget that I am not a boy."

That was a hard duty to impose on the pastor, who looked into the browned face and the troubled dark eyes. He did not promise, but simply said, "The class, as you heard, will meet in the dining-room at the parsonage on Wednesday afternoon. I hope the instructions may be blessed to you," and they parted.

Wednesday came. The available chairs in the pastor's simple home had been ranged in long rows on each side of the dining-room.

"May I sit here, dear, with my work?" said the pastor's wife, coming in with a basket of stockings in one hand, her needle

Mrs. Woods Baker

and yarn for darning in the other.

She did not expect to be refused, nor was she, though a little girl of five years old, her only child, held pertinaciously on to her dress. "I may come too, papa; I am sure I may," said a sweet, cheery voice, and only a pleasant smile was the reply. The mother sat down in one of the chairs still at the table, and the little girl took joyously a place at her side.

"I always like to hear your confirmation instructions, for many reasons," said the wife. "I seem to take a fresh start in the right direction with the children."

The pastor seated himself at the head of the table, with his books before him, laying near them the list of the names of the class.

The pastor was a stout, sensible-looking man, with a plain, quiet face, and a modest, shy air. Indeed, he was hardly at ease anywhere, except in his home, or in the pulpit or chancel, where the sense of the sacredness of his official duties made him unmindful of earthly witnesses.

Now he thought it a stay to have his wife with him; for the informal nature of the meeting, and the beginning of something new, made the whole at first an effort for him.

Perhaps the pastor, in the presence of persons of high standing, found it impossible to forget his humble birth, and suspected that in some way there was always a lack of gentility about him; while with companions of more modest pretensions he must maintain the distant dignity which he fancied appertained to his profession.

He was a straightforward, matter-of-fact man, who intended in all things, temporal and spiritual, to do his duty. He believed fully in the inspiration of the Bible from cover to cover, and was possibly convinced that every word, and almost every letter, in the then authorized Swedish version had a sanction not to be disputed. In his view the sacraments, properly administered, were direct, undoubted channels of grace. The organization of his church was perfect, he was sure, to the least particular, and would have the approval of the apostles were they now on earth, though during their lives the circumstances of their surroundings might have made it impossible for them to have their ministrations conducted according to the admirable order so long established in Sweden. Martin Luther he looked upon as having a kind of supplemental apostleship, almost as incontestable as that of Peter himself. Luther's catechism was for him the best medium for imparting religious instruction to children, and for strengthening the Christian life of young people approaching maturity. With this sound, hearty belief in what he was called on to teach, and with the rules for his ministrations, his work was simple and most agreeable.

The pastor was not an emotional man. He had never been deeply stirred by religious feelings of any kind. He had had no agonies of penitence, no distressing doubts, no strong struggles with temper, no vivid thought of the possibility of his being excluded from eternal blessedness. His heavenly Father was to him rather a theological abstraction than a near and ever-loving friend. The Saviour was to him more an element in a perfect creed than the Deliverer—the hand stretched out to the drowning man—the one hope of poor tempted humanity.

The pastor was, in his way, a good man, a kind man, an unselfish, true, sincere man. Peaceful he lived, peaceful he ministered, and yet heart to heart he came with no human brother. With no human brother, we say; but there was one woman whose life interpenetrated his, if they did not in all things come heart to heart. Her presence gave him a sense of sunshine and quiet happiness that was the greatest joy of which his nature was capable.

Merry, impulsive, devoted, self-sacrificing by nature, the whole existence of the pastor's wife was pervaded by a Christian life that exalted her naturally lovely traits, and made her shortcomings the source of a sweet, childlike penitence that was almost as lovely and attractive as her virtues. She had soon found that the deep language of her inner soul was to her husband an unknown tongue. Of her spiritual struggles and joys and exaltations she did not speak to him or to any other human being. They were her secret with her God and Saviour. Yet her husband stood to her on a pinnacle, as rounded in character, blameless in life, and perfect in his ministrations. Almost angelic he seemed to her when he stood in the chancel, and in his deep, melodious voice sang all the parts of the service that the church rules allowed to be so given.

The pastor's sermons were excellent compositions. Compositions they were in the strictest sense of the word. The epistles and gospels for the ecclesiastical year were the authorized and usual subjects for the sermons, being called even in common parlance "the text for the day." These texts had been so elaborated and expounded by wise divines whose works were to be had in print, that when a sermon was to be written, our pastor but got out his books of sermons, studied, compared, compiled, extracted, transformed, and rewrote, until on Friday his sermon for the coming Sunday was always ready. He had made it his own by hard, conscientious work, and not without a deep sense that he was, in his way, to deliver a divine message as an authorized ambassador of the King of kings, accredited and appointed in an unimpeachable manner.

With his confirmation class the pastor was different. He was fond of young people. He had been young himself, and had not forgotten the circumstance.

He was getting a little impatient to see the fresh faces he was expecting at the first meeting of the class, when Johanson made his appearance, bowed distantly, and took the seat nearest the door. He had passed through a knot of young people without, who were, with some cuffing and shoving, contending who should go in first on this to them august occasion. Johanson had left the door slightly ajar, and little Elsa, the pastor's child, having caught a glimpse of a familiar face, ran out, to come back immediately leading triumphantly a rosy-cheeked girl, who was all blushes as she was brought into the dining-room, made to her for the time sacred ground. Of course, the whole troop from without, boys and girls, followed, taking opposite sides of the room.

It proved that Johanson had taken his seat on the girls' side, and carefully away from him the skirts of those nearest to him were drawn; for it had been whispered around the parish that the queer man at the poorhouse had never been confirmed. An outcast of the outcasts he must be, was the common conviction.

A hymn was to be sung, all sitting, to open the meeting. Little Elsa went round with the "psalm-books" in a basket, and began with Johanson, who took one as he was requested. The pastor began, and the young voices joined him. There was a hush for a second, when a wonderful tenor came in, and seemed to fill the room with a strange melody.

But one verse was sung; then followed a short prayer from the church liturgy, after which the lesson began.

Johanson sat alone in his corner, when Elsa tripped away

Mrs. Woods Baker

from her mother, and giving a gleeful little hop, she seated herself beside him, laid her small hand lightly on his knee, and looked up at him lovingly and protectingly as she did so. Now she felt she really owned him. He was *her* poor man, a kind of friend and relation to her.

Through all those long preparatory lessons Elsa kept her place by the side of the dark man, without word or comment from her parents.

The time for the confirmation was drawing near. "I do not know what I shall do about Johanson," said the pastor to his wife. "I get nothing from him in the class except plain, direct, and most correct answers to my questions. I suppose it must be all right, but we don't seem to come near to each other at all. He is a wild, strange man. Perhaps you could somehow get on better with him."

"Maybe Elsa could," said the wife. "*She* loves him. Perhaps that is what he feels the need of among us who call ourselves Christians."

"Call ourselves Christians!" repeated the pastor, in as severe a tone of reproach as he had ever addressed to his wife.

She did not seem to notice his manner, but went on: "Elsa might reach him. You know it says, 'A little child shall lead them.' I'll send her to the poorhouse this afternoon with a message to Johanson from me, and the book she likes so much. I know which is her favourite picture, and she will be sure to tell him about it."

"Send her to the poorhouse!" exclaimed the pastor.

"She's been there often with me when I've been there to wind up Gull's clock, which she is sure to get out of order if Gull touches it herself. Elsa is not afraid of any of them, even of the cellar-master. He really likes her."

The pastor was called away suddenly, and he was glad, for that was one of the occasions when he did not quite understand his wife.

Mrs. Woods Baker

CHAPTER V

LED TO THE LIGHT

Little Elsa's errand to Johanson was to take to him a small pocket "psalm-book" (as the Swedish book for the services and hymns is called). It was well known in the poorhouse and parish that the stranger pauper had a Bible, and read it too, at least for five minutes every day. Gull, who had a strong taste for gossip, had not left that particular unmentioned.

Elsa came in with two little packages in her hand. "Here's your book mamma sent you," she said. "She has put your name in it. I want to show you my book too."

Johanson put his gift in his pocket hastily, with a short expression of thanks, and then looked expectantly at the child.

"May I sit close to you, so we can both look over it together?" she said, as she pushed a chair to his side and worked herself up on to it.

The illustrations were generally from Old Testament scenes; but Elsa hurried past these, turning the pages briskly with her skilful fingers.

"Here it is! Here's the one I like best. You understand it, don't you? It means something," and she looked up questioningly into his face.

The picture was a most admirable representation of the Good Shepherd bearing a lost lamb home on His shoulders.

Johanson was silent.

"You don't know about it, then? I will tell you," she said, and went on, while her tiny finger was impressively pointing from lamb to shepherd, and from shepherd to lamb.

"That little lamb got far away from the shepherd and the fold and all the little lambs he knew. And he was dirty, not a bit clean, and his wool was all torn by the briers, and the thorns had hurt him, and he was hungry and thirsty and tired, and did not know where to go. He could hear the wolves growl, and he thought he could see their eyes looking at him as if they wanted to eat him up. You see he had run away, just gone away from the Good Shepherd and his mother and his home, when he did not need to. And now he wanted to get back, but he didn't know how; and then he began to complain and to bleat (that's his way of crying), and to run this way and that, but he didn't get on at all.

"At last he was quite tired out, and he thought he must give up and lie down and die where he was. Then the Good Shepherd heard his cry and came to him. The poor little lamb wanted to follow the Shepherd; but he was too weak—he could hardly stand alone. And then"—and here the little voice grew triumphantly glad—"then the Good Shepherd took him in His own arms, just as sweet and kind as if the naughty lamb had never run away, and carried him over the stones, and past the briers, and across the little streams, and up the steep hills, and through the dark places! He carried

Mrs. Woods Baker

him *all the way* home, not just half-way and then let him drop. He carried him *all the way home* to the fold, where his mother was, and there he was safe—safe—safe! Wasn't that a Good Shepherd?"

There was no answer.

"My mother told me all about it, and I like that picture best and that story best. You understand what it means?"

"Yes," said Johanson. There were tears in his eyes.

Elsa lifted up her loving hand to Johanson's face as it was bent over the book, and with her own little handkerchief wiped his tears; then she went out silently, which was probably the best thing she could have done under the circumstances.

The next day Johanson went to the pastor in his study. "I have not come to talk about *my* fitness for confirmation," he said. "Little Elsa has taught me better. I have turned my face towards the Good Shepherd, and I believe He will carry me home. May I meet with the class to-morrow?"

"Certainly," said the pastor, and the interview was ended.

Johanson sat among the candidates for confirmation the next day—among the boys and girls, like a battered old ship that had been dragged into the harbour beside the trim fresh vessels just starting with flying colours for a bright far-away land.

He did not mind the nudges and half-smiles among the rustic congregation, but answered the questions put to him with the others, in his strong man's voice, as simply and naturally as a child.

He knew he was safe in the hands of the Good Shepherd, who would carry him tenderly home, and his heart was full of humble joy.

The administration of the holy communion took place next day. The newly-confirmed with their friends were to "go forward," while the rest of the congregation were to remain in their seats praying for the young soldiers of Christ, now fully enlisted under His banner.

Johanson had taken a modest place at the chancel railing; but even there he was an outcast, for it was plain that no one was willing to kneel beside him.

The pastor's wife was bowed low with new food for prayer and thanksgiving. Little Elsa moved quickly from her mother's side up the aisle, and to the astonishment and almost horror of the congregation she knelt by Johanson, her little head not appearing above the railing; but she held fast to his left hand. He felt the tender familiar grasp, and it was to him like the Good Shepherd greeting him through one of His little ones.

At the close of the service, when all the authorized words for the occasion had been read, the pastor stepped to the front of the chancel, and said, in loud, clear tones,—

"And the father saw him afar off, and ran and fell on his neck, and kissed him." "Him that cometh to me I will in no wise cast out." "A broken and a contrite heart, O God, thou wilt not despise." "Come unto me, all ye that labour and are heavy laden, and I will give you rest."

"I hope it was not amiss to say those words I did from the chancel to-day," said the pastor to his wife when at home and they were alone together. "They are not in the service, but I

Mrs. Woods Baker

could not help it. I never felt so deeply before how freely and fully God forgives us—*us* Christians as well as what we call 'poor sinners.' Yes, it came over me as it never has before, and somehow heaven seems nearer, and God more really my Father and Christ my Saviour. Do you understand me, my dear?"

"Yes, yes," she said—"yes, dear; and you too seem nearer to me than ever before."

The pastor answered, tenderly and solemnly: "It is you, wife, you and Elsa, and that poor Johanson, who have somehow opened my eyes. I have seen before, but seen darkly. May God lead me to the perfect day!"

CHAPTER VI

PAINFUL DISCLOSURES

Something about the strange inmate had affected the mad poet, long a dweller in the poorhouse, as unusual in that establishment. These fancies he had versified, and having written the result down on a half-sheet of paper, he folded it into a narrow strip, and then twisted it into an almost impossible knot, and handed it to the person nearest concerned.

Johanson read with astonishment:—

It striketh me
That you should be
A gentleman,
And drive a span,
Live high, drink wine,
Ask folks to dine,
And make a dash.
With poorhouse trash
You should not be—
With folks like me."

In return, the reply was promptly put under the poor poet's door:—

Mrs. Woods Baker

"Of who I am, or where belong,
Please do not whisper in your song."

These communications were followed by a few days of unusual silence between the neighbours. The mad poet did not like being answered in rhyme. Of versification he considered himself the inventor, and as having therefore an exclusive right to use it, in conversation or on paper.

At last Johanson made up his mind what course to pursue in the matter. He went to the poet in a friendly way, and said to him, "I take you to be a gentleman who knows how to keep a secret, and does not mention what he can guess out concerning other people's matters. I know your principles about your post-bag. I have heard that you never even read the address of a letter to be sent off, or the post-mark of one to be delivered. Now I call that a high sense of honour."

"Just decency
It seems to me,"

broke in the poet.

Johanson did not seem to notice the interruption, but went on: "Now you keep anything you suspect about me, anything you can't understand in my ways, just as secret as if it were written on the back of a letter. You will, I am sure. So now let us shake hands upon it." They did, and were established as better friends than before.

The weather had become extremely cold, but the poorhouse poet went on his rounds, persisting in being dressed as in the autumn.

It had been snowing all night, and the cold was excessive. Johanson was awakened by an unusual chill in the air. A long point of snow lay along the floor of his room, as it had drifted in under the not over-tight door. He dressed and hurried out. The vestibule was one snow-bank, and the outside door was wide open. He pushed his way into the poet's room. It was empty. It was plain that the poor fellow had been out on his usual rounds, and had not returned to put up the outer bars, as was his nightly custom; for the old locks were not to be relied upon. He probably had not been able to force his way through the heavy drifts and the wild storm which was still raging.

The cellar-master was a late sleeper. He woke now to see Johanson hurrying about, evidently making ready for a trip.

"What are you doing? You are letting the cold in here, sir," said the old fellow, only half awake.

"The poet is missing. He didn't come home last night. I shall go and look him up. Have you any whisky? You have, I know. I saw Gull bring you in a bottle last night. Let me have it, will you?"

"Yes; a pull will keep you up," was the answer.

"I don't want it for me," said Johanson hastily; "it has pulled me down low enough. I'll never taste it again. But that poor fellow, he may need it, if I find him."

"You are not going to risk yourself out looking for *him*!" said the cellar-master, now fairly awake. "*You* are right down crazy. Quiet yourself. He'll be coming in soon, and making rhymes about his trip. You don't look over hearty. I should think you would be afraid to risk it."

"Afraid!" said Johanson. "Have you ever been in a tornado? Have you been in an earthquake? Have you been out in a

Mrs. Woods Baker

blizzard, with no house within miles?"

"No, no, no!" was the threefold reply.

"I've tried them all," said Johanson, "and I am not afraid of a little snow. Lend me your stick, and I'm off."

Off he was, but not to return through the long morning. Towards noon, a party who had been out with a snow-plough and a sledge came back, bearing two bodies carefully covered.

The poet was still and white. He had been found lying under a rock, in a tiny natural cave. On a ledge near him, in some lightly-sifted snow, he had traced with his finger:—

"I must be ill,
I've such a chill.
Here I'll die,
Nobody by.
Who'll cry?
Not I!
The bag'll be found,
It's safe and sound.
There'll be no snow
Where I shall go;
There'll be no storm,
It will be warm.
Good-night!
Good-night!"

It was good-night indeed for the poorhouse poet. In his pocket was found a worn scrap of paper, on which was pencilled his simple creed:—

"The tickets buy

For when we die,
For where we go
We fix below.
Death clears the track;
We can't come back!

"Somehow, I guess,
If we confess,
And say, 'Forgive!'
Up there we'll live.
Conductors quail,
And kings prevail.
When God has said,
'Alive or dead,
I own that man,'
He save him can."

In Johanson there still was life. He had been found lying close to the dead poet, as if trying to share with him his little remaining vital warmth. The doctor, the pastor's wife, and Gull were soon doing all that was possible to call him back to life. In a few days he was almost well, for broken down though he was, he still had some of the vigour of his naturally strong constitution.

The funeral was over. Johanson was apparently dozing, lying on his sofa, now in its form for the day; while Gull and the cellar-master were chatting together in low, whispering tones.

Gull, who had prepared the body of the poorhouse poet for interment, now talked over all the items of the expense with evident satisfaction, and concluded by saying, "It was a beautiful corpse. It really was a pleasure to lay him out, he looked so sweet and quiet when it was all done."

Mrs. Woods Baker

The cellar-master, who had been helped into a sleigh to attend, remarked that it was a charming funeral; he did not know when he had enjoyed himself so much as on the late occasion.

"What luck he had to come in for the bell!" said Gull; "he was just in the nick of time. It was really quite a grand funeral, with the three coffins—the baby and the old woman and our young man—and the mourners for all. The pastor did it beautiful too, and the bell sounded so solemn. It is, of course, another thing when the big bell is rung for some high body that is carried out. We may be thankful that we have the little bell rung once a week for poor folks' funerals in this parish; it is not so everywhere."

"It would seem more solemn to see the pastor in his black gloves if he didn't wear them always," said the cellar-master. "Why does he do it? I never happened to meet anybody that knew. He's still-like himself, and nobody likes to ask him questions. Some people say it is to make him look grand with fine folks, and to kind of put down them that have bare hands used to work."

"Don't you know about his hands?" asked Gull, with surprise. "I've known it so many years, it seems as if everybody must have heard that."

"I don't happen to have inquired into the matter," said the cellar-master, somewhat humiliated. "I have never been one to gossip."

"Why, I was there when it happened," broke out Gull, eager to tell her story to a new listener. "He was stable-boy when I was housemaid at the major's. My lady was sitting in the carriage one day, and Lars—we called him Lars then—was standing holding the horses. My lady had sent the coachman in for his cape, for it was getting cold—just like her. The horses took fright at a travelling music-man who came along, and must begin just then to play. Off they started full run, dragging Lars, who hung on to the reins until they stopped. He'd have held on to those reins, I'm sure, till he died (what he began he always stuck to); and my lady sitting there in the carriage half scared to death. The fingers on his left hand were cut to the bones. They were long healing, and a sight to be seen then at the best. The right wasn't much better, dragged along the road as it had been. My lady always liked Lars after that. He had always been for reading; and when he took it into his head he wanted to be a priest, she helped him, and other folks helped him too. He changed his name, as poor fellows do when they go to Upsala. When my lady and the major were taken off so sudden with the fever, he kept on at his learning. He wouldn't have given up if he'd had to starve. But he didn't, for one way and another he got on. And then what a wife he picked up, and a little money with her too; not that it's enough to wipe out old scores. Those Upsala debts hang after him, as they have after many another. He's got them all in one hand now, they say, so that he hasn't to pay on them more than once a year, and that time is just coming on. You can see it in him as well as you can see in the west when there'll be snow next morning. He's rubbed through so far, but it sits heavy. I'm not in their kitchen for an odd bit of work now and then for nothing. I see what I see, and I hear what I hear. Beda is lonely like, and she's pleased to have somebody to talk out to. What if the pastor and his wife should find out who's who!" she continued, pointing over her shoulder at the supposed sleeper.

The cellar-master gave a stupid look at her mysterious face.

"That's the major's son over there," she whispered—"Alf, who ran off and never came back. I must tell somebody, if I should die for it. But you mustn't breathe it to a living soul."

Mrs. Woods Baker

"Not that beautiful young fellow! No, no; you don't make me believe that. Don't I remember him? This one isn't a bit like him—an ugly, worthless-looking old tramp. He was a wild chap, Alf. My wife used to tell me it was a shame to let him come there and drink—drink down a glass as if he couldn't swallow it quick enough, and then another, and then go out to the stable-boy, who was there to help him home. But that's not Alf. I'd know that handsome fellow anywhere among a million."

"But that *is* Alf," she whispered. "When he was almost frozen to death, the doctor told me to open his breast and rub him well; and I did. But what did I find there, hanging on to a black string, but his mother's picture, in a little locket she gave him when he was a little fellow; and he was so fond of it then he would wear it outside his clothes, where everybody could see, he said. He's willing enough to hide it now; he don't want to shame such parents, and that's the only good thing I see about him. I found it out, and I know it; but I won't tell anybody but you."

"That's Alf! And I helped to make him so! My wife said I'd rue the day. Now I do. It's very fine to be called 'cellar-master' when you sit fast in the poorhouse; but it's a bad business dragging people down. Think what Alf was and see what he is! I don't want to talk any more to-day. You go, Gull. I've got something to think about."

Johanson, lost in his own thoughts, had not noticed the whispered conversation till his own name of the past was mentioned. After that, in bitter repentance he heard the galling words that penetrated his inmost soul. Now he understood Gull's new politeness to him, and the kindly willingness with which she saved him in his degradation, for his mother's sake. She could not treat him like a common tenant of the poorhouse, and he was sure she would keep his secret. With the cellar-master it might be a different thing. That his companions knew him was an added humiliation. He had deserved it all; but there was One who had called Himself the Friend of sinners, and that Friend had received even him, a poor prodigal who had returned to his Father's house.

CHAPTER VII

A HAPPY CHRISTMAS

The pastor had fallen into the pleasant habit of having his wife with him when he wrote his sermons. Alone in the morning he made his researches and his copious notes for his compilation. In the evening he talked over with his wife the subject in hand, before the work of writing really began. She found him one night, shortly before Christmas, sitting dolorously before his table covered with papers, while an unusual cloud overshadowed his face.

"I cannot even think how to begin, wife," he said; "my thoughts will run in quite another direction. I feel all the weight of the new year upon me. Those old debts of mine, that I can never hope to clear off, hang upon me like a hopeless weight. A few years less at Upsala, and a good deal less debt, would have been a far better preparation for such a parish as this."

The pastor's wife was not at all cast down by this sorrowful lament. It had long been a familiar strain to her. She answered cheerily,—

"You had nothing to do with the arrangements as to what you were to learn at Upsala, and how long you must be there.

You worked hard, and denied yourself almost the necessaries of life, as you well know. Now you are here and at your higher mission, which *must* be faithfully performed. So you will have to throw all these cares overboard. Just when we are to remember that 'God so loved the world,' we must not forget that He loves us still, every one of us. We here in this little parsonage are under His care, and He is not going to let us have burdens heavier than we can bear. We live simply enough; there is no faring 'sumptuously every day' here, as all the parish knows. I have thought out a little help. We will not give each other anything for Christmas. If gifts are but an expression of love, we do not need that kind of expression between us. For Elsa I have made a big rag doll, dressed in a fine peasant dress, from the scraps in my piece-bag. We will have a little Christmas-tree on a table for a variety, and I have put tinsel round nuts to hang upon it with the pretty red apples from the garden; and as to candles, we have enough left from last year. We will all learn that beautiful carol we had sent us by mail yesterday. Our good Beda, she must not be disappointed. I have my uncle's last present to me in money, which I shall share with her, and give her the dress from my aunt that I have not yet made up for myself. The rest of aunty's present will do to make Christmas cheery for the poorhouse people and the hard-pinched folks in the parish, who look for a little from us at this time. So now all those troublesome matters are blown away. As for the interest on the old debts, that is not to be paid until January; and we will leave that to the loving Lord, who has given us so many blessings, and see now after the sermon with cheerful, thankful hearts. Come, dear; now I am ready to hear about it."

And they did begin on the sermon, and it was the best the pastor had ever written. Something of the sweet cheerfulness and loving gratitude of the wife had made its way among the sound theological quotations and the judicious

Mrs. Woods Baker

condensations. There was new life in the whole, which now came really from the pastor's uplifted soul, and would find its way to the stirred hearts of the hearers.

Christmas morning came, and little Elsa was early at the poorhouse. She had a present for Johanson. It was but a bit of work on perforated paper, done by her own hands—a lamb outlined in gay silk; but it was a *lamb*, and she felt that meant something between her and Johanson, and it did.

He was moved when he took it, and thanked her with good wishes for Christmas from the depths of his heart.

"I am so happy, Johanson," she said, "for papa and mamma are so glad. I heard them say, 'Now the past is all wiped away, and we can begin the new year as free from care as the birds.' I have often heard mamma say that the past is all, all wiped away when we are sorry for what we have done and want to do better, and I am always so glad about that. But this, I am sure, meant something different; for they said something about a letter, and then they looked together at a paper as if they could kiss it, and said, 'We must thank God for it, and ask Him to bless an unknown friend with His best blessings.' And they just talked to God where they sat, as they do sometimes. Papa has been sorrowful lately, but he really looked to-day like mamma when she is the happiest."

The child had found Johanson bowed, sitting with his head in his hands, while his thoughts were far back in his sinful, sorrowful past. He had felt as if he had hardly a right to welcome the day when the Saviour was born. Now his face beamed with joy; but he only said, "I am glad you are all so happy. I am sure you will be pleased again when you see something in church to-day."

Many weeks before Christmas, Johanson had asked

permission to go into the church, and to have a tall ladder carried in with him. The pastor was astonished at the request. The permission had been granted. No results of the matter had, however, appeared. The same permission had been given the day before. There had been some hammering then, he understood, but had no misgivings in the matter, as he had begun to trust Johanson as an upright, honest man.

There were surprise and delight on all faces when they entered the church for the early service on Christmas morning. Of course there was a perfect blaze of light within, but that they had expected. The golden cross was gone; the red curtain had disappeared; the old picture, now but a ragged canvas, had been removed, and in its place was a beautiful painting. It represented the Lord Jesus, sitting with a glory round His benign countenance, welcoming a penitent, weary pilgrim from afar, who knelt to receive His blessing. Below was the legend, "Him that cometh to Me I will in no wise cast out."

The carol that was sung was the same that the pastor's wife had chosen to be used at the lighting of the tree in her own home the evening before. The rural choir had practised it well, and it sounded out over the old church like angelic music.

At the first notes Johanson started and covered his face with his hands. A moment later, though he held no notes to follow, his beautiful voice rang out loud and clear and in full harmony with the other singers.

When the service was over, there was a crowd lingering in the aisles, praising and admiring the beautiful picture and the new carol; but Johanson was soon alone in the poorhouse, with "Hosanna! hosanna!" in his heart.

Mrs. Woods Baker

CHAPTER VIII

THE BEATA CHARITY

Gull had come to the cellar-master with a choice bit of news to tell. A stranger had bought the land where the major's home and stood, and buildings were to be put up there immediately. The long lonely spot was soon a busy scene, as the architect, with plans in hand, was hurrying about among the skilful workmen.

Whoever would, might hear where the new poorhouse was to stand, and where the orphan home, and know that the little red cottage, just like any other, was for a musical composer, who must have one large room built with special care and according to all the most scientific acoustic rules; for there he was to have a fine organ, which was now being constructed in the most particular manner. "I want to call it all 'The Beata Charity,' for Beata was my mother's name," Johanson had said to the pastor, who was now in his full confidence. They knew each other as the Alf and Lars of the olden time. They knew each other now as forgiven sinners, each striving in his own way to work for the glory of the Master's kingdom. Each felt that he was indebted to the other. The stable-boy's words, "The duties are the same whether you make the promises or not," had lingered in the mind of the wanderer in the midst of the lowest depths of sin, and had brought him home at last to try *to make the promises firmly resolved to keep them.*

The methodical, authorized, ordained, instructed, conscientious priest had learned from a repentant sinner to bow at the foot of the Cross, and thank God for the Saviour who could forgive him his poor, blind, cold, self-satisfied service of the past, and wake him to penitence and love, and humble, grateful faithfulness in his sacred office.

Johanson's work in the poorhouse on his music-paper had been the solace of those long, dark penitential hours. His alternations between deep depression and dawning hope, and at last his full, deep conviction that there was pardon for all in the abundant mercy of God through Christ, had been expressed in the musical compositions that had made their way over the length and breadth of the land.

Many of them were linked with old familiar sacred words; for others, some master-poet must be warmed to write their language in glowing verse.

"The white-haired pauper," as Johanson was called throughout the whole country, had his satisfaction in his life-long incognito. He felt that he had cast aside his old name and old privileges to be a worthless wanderer, and had but returned to repent and be forgiven. He would, himself forgotten and unknown, praise and serve as God had given him ability.

The grand-uncle in America, so munificent for Alf's confirmation day, had always cherished a hope of the prodigal's reformation. Only when in desperate need had Alf applied to him, and had never been refused assistance. Dying, the old man had left a will bequeathing his large fortune to his grand-nephew, in the firm belief that Alf, having run his wild career, would find his way to his native land, to lead a faithful Christian life, and be the centre of wide benevolent enterprises.

The hopes and wishes and prayers of the uncle were fulfilled. The white-haired pauper lived to see the results of his efforts, and to know that many who starving had been fed, or sinning reclaimed, or suffering ministered unto, were calling down blessings on his unworthy head.

From the pastor and his wife and Elsa Alf had sympathy and aid in all his undertakings, and their friendship was cemented by common work for the common good.

The cellar-master did not live to have a place in the new poorhouse. Gull had her own trial in the midst of the comforts of her old age, that she must still keep the secret that the celebrated composer and wide philanthropist was her beloved "major's" long-lost son.

THE END

Choose from Thousands of 1stWorldLibrary Classics By

A. M. Barnard	Booth Tarkington	Edward Everett Hale
Ada Leverson	Boyd Cable	Edward J. O'Brien
Adolphus William Ward	Bram Stoker	Edward S. Ellis
Aesop	C. Collodi	Edwin L. Arnold
Agatha Christie	C. E. Orr	Eleanor Atkins
Alexander Aaronsohn	C. M. Ingleby	Eleanor Hallowell Abbott
Alexander Kielland	Carolyn Wells	Eliot Gregory
Alexandre Dumas	Catherine Parr Traill	Elizabeth Gaskell
Alfred Gatty	Charles A. Eastman	Elizabeth McCracken
Alfred Ollivant	Charles Amory Beach	Elizabeth Von Arnim
Alice Duer Miller	Charles Dickens	Ellem Key
Alice Turner Curtis	Charles Dudley Warner	Emerson Hough
Alice Dunbar	Charles Farrar Browne	Emilie F. Carlen
Allen Chapman	Charles Ives	Emily Bronte
Alleyne Ireland	Charles Kingsley	Emily Dickinson
Ambrose Bierce	Charles Klein	Enid Bagnold
Amelia E. Barr	Charles Hanson Towne	Enilor Macartney Lane
Amory H. Bradford	Charles Lathrop Pack	Erasmus W. Jones
Andrew Lang	Charles Romyn Dake	Ernie Howard Pie
Andrew McFarland Davis	Charles Whibley	Ethel May Dell
Andy Adams	Charles Willing Beale	Ethel Turner
Angela Brazil	Charlotte M. Braeme	Ethel Watts Mumford
Anna Alice Chapin	Charlotte M. Yonge	Eugene Sue
Anna Sewell	Charlotte Perkins Stetson	Eugenie Foa
Annie Besant	Clair W. Hayes	Eugene Wood
Annie Hamilton Donnell	Clarence Day Jr.	Eustace Hale Ball
Annie Payson Call	Clarence E. Mulford	Evelyn Everett-green
Annie Roe Carr	Clemence Housman	Everard Cotes
Annonaymous	Confucius	F. H. Cheley
Anton Chekhov	Coningsby Dawson	F. J. Cross
Archibald Lee Fletcher	Cornelis DeWitt Wilcox	F. Marion Crawford
Arnold Bennett	Cyril Burleigh	Fannie E. Newberry
Arthur C. Benson	D. H. Lawrence	Federick Austin Ogg
Arthur Conan Doyle	Daniel Defoe	Ferdinand Ossendowski
Arthur M. Winfield	David Garnett	Fergus Hume
Arthur Ransome	Dinah Craik	Florence A. Kilpatrick
Arthur Schnitzler	Don Carlos Janes	Fremont B. Deering
Arthur Train	Donald Keyhoe	Francis Bacon
Atticus	Dorothy Kilner	Francis Darwin
B.H. Baden-Powell	Dougan Clark	Frances Hodgson Burnett
B. M. Bower	Douglas Fairbanks	Frances Parkinson Keyes
B. C. Chatterjee	E. Nesbit	Frank Gee Patchin
Baroness Emmuska Orczy	E. P. Roe	Frank Harris
Baroness Orczy	E. Phillips Oppenheim	Frank Jewett Mather
Basil King	E. S. Brooks	Frank L. Packard
Bayard Taylor	Earl Barnes	Frank V. Webster
Ben Macomber	Edgar Rice Burroughs	Frederic Stewart Isham
Bertha Muzzy Bower	Edith Van Dyne	Frederick Trevor Hill
Bjornstjerne Bjornson	Edith Wharton	Frederick Winslow Taylor

Friedrich Kerst
Friedrich Nietzsche
Fyodor Dostoyevsky
G.A. Henty
G.K. Chesterton
Gabrielle E. Jackson
Garrett P. Serviss
Gaston Leroux
George A. Warren
George Ade
Geroge Bernard Shaw
George Cary Eggleston
George Durston
George Ebers
George Eliot
George Gissing
George MacDonald
George Meredith
George Orwell
George Sylvester Viereck
George Tucker
George W. Cable
George Wharton James
Gertrude Atherton
Gordon Casserly
Grace E. King
Grace Gallatin
Grace Greenwood
Grant Allen
Guillermo A. Sherwell
Gulielma Zollinger
Gustav Flaubert
H. A. Cody
H. B. Irving
H.C. Bailey
H. G. Wells
H. H. Munro
H. Irving Hancock
H. R. Naylor
H. Rider Haggard
H. W. C. Davis
Haldeman Julius
Hall Caine
Hamilton Wright Mabie
Hans Christian Andersen
Harold Avery
Harold McGrath
Harriet Beecher Stowe
Harry Castlemon
Harry Coghill
Harry Houidini

Hayden Carruth
Helent Hunt Jackson
Helen Nicolay
Hendrik Conscience
Hendy David Thoreau
Henri Barbusse
Henrik Ibsen
Henry Adams
Henry Ford
Henry Frost
Henry James
Henry Jones Ford
Henry Seton Merriman
Henry W Longfellow
Herbert A. Giles
Herbert Carter
Herbert N. Casson
Herman Hesse
Hildegard G. Frey
Homer
Honore De Balzac
Horace B. Day
Horace Walpole
Horatio Alger Jr.
Howard Pyle
Howard R. Garis
Hugh Lofting
Hugh Walpole
Humphry Ward
Ian Maclaren
Inez Haynes Gillmore
Irving Bacheller
Isabel Cecilia Williams
Isabel Hornibrook
Israel Abrahams
Ivan Turgenev
J.G.Austin
J. Henri Fabre
J. M. Barrie
J. M. Walsh
J. Macdonald Oxley
J. R. Miller
J. S. Fletcher
J. S. Knowles
J. Storer Clouston
J. W. Duffield
Jack London
Jacob Abbott
James Allen
James Andrews
James Baldwin

James Branch Cabell
James DeMille
James Joyce
James Lane Allen
James Lane Allen
James Oliver Curwood
James Oppenheim
James Otis
James R. Driscoll
Jane Abbott
Jane Austen
Jane L. Stewart
Janet Aldridge
Jens Peter Jacobsen
Jerome K. Jerome
Jessie Graham Flower
John Buchan
John Burroughs
John Cournos
John F. Kennedy
John Gay
John Glasworthy
John Habberton
John Joy Bell
John Kendrick Bangs
John Milton
John Philip Sousa
John Taintor Foote
Jonas Lauritz Idemil Lie
Jonathan Swift
Joseph A. Altsheler
Joseph Carey
Joseph Conrad
Joseph E. Badger Jr
Joseph Hergesheimer
Joseph Jacobs
Jules Vernes
Julian Hawthrone
Julie A Lippmann
Justin Huntly McCarthy
Kakuzo Okakura
Karle Wilson Baker
Kate Chopin
Kenneth Grahame
Kenneth McGaffey
Kate Langley Bosher
Kate Langley Bosher
Katherine Cecil Thurston
Katherine Stokes
L. A. Abbot
L. T. Meade

L. Frank Baum	Paul G. Tomlinson	T. S. Arthur
Latta Griswold	Paul Severing	The Princess Der Ling
Laura Dent Crane	Percy Brebner	Thomas A. Janvier
Laura Lee Hope	Percy Keese Fitzhugh	Thomas A Kempis
Laurence Housman	Peter B. Kyne	Thomas Anderton
Lawrence Beasley	Plato	Thomas Bailey Aldrich
Leo Tolstoy	Quincy Allen	Thomas Bulfinch
Leonid Andreyev	R. Derby Holmes	Thomas De Quincey
Lewis Carroll	R. L. Stevenson	Thomas Dixon
Lewis Sperry Chafer	R. S. Ball	Thomas H. Huxley
Lilian Bell	Rabindranath Tagore	Thomas Hardy
Lloyd Osbourne	Rahul Alvares	Thomas More
Louis Hughes	Ralph Bonehill	Thornton W. Burgess
Louis Joseph Vance	Ralph Henry Barbour	U. S. Grant
Louis Tracy	Ralph Victor	Upton Sinclair
Louisa May Alcott	Ralph Waldo Emmerson	Valentine Williams
Lucy Fitch Perkins	Rene Descartes	Various Authors
Lucy Maud Montgomery	Ray Cummings	Vaughan Kester
Luther Benson	Rex Beach	Victor Appleton
Lydia Miller Middleton	Rex E. Beach	Victor G. Durham
Lyndon Orr	Richard Harding Davis	Victoria Cross
M. Corvus	Richard Jefferies	Virginia Woolf
M. H. Adams	Richard Le Gallienne	Wadsworth Camp
Margaret E. Sangster	Robert Barr	Walter Camp
Margret Howth	Robert Frost	Walter Scott
Margaret Vandercook	Robert Gordon Anderson	Washington Irving
Margaret W. Hungerford	Robert L. Drake	Wilbur Lawton
Margret Penrose	Robert Lansing	Wilkie Collins
Maria Edgeworth	Robert Lynd	Willa Cather
Maria Thompson Daviess	Robert Michael Ballantyne	Willard F. Baker
Mariano Azuela	Robert W. Chambers	William Dean Howells
Marion Polk Angellotti	Rosa Nouchette Carey	William le Queux
Mark Overton	Rudyard Kipling	W. Makepeace Thackeray
Mark Twain	Saint Augustine	William W. Walter
Mary Austin	Samuel B. Allison	William Shakespeare
Mary Catherine Crowley	Samuel Hopkins Adams	Winston Churchill
Mary Cole	Sarah Bernhardt	Yei Theodora Ozaki
Mary Hastings Bradley	Sarah C. Hallowell	Yogi Ramacharaka
Mary Roberts Rinehart	Selma Lagerlof	Young E. Allison
Mary Rowlandson	Sherwood Anderson	Zane Grey
M. Wollstonecraft Shelley	Sigmund Freud	
Maud Lindsay	Standish O'Grady	
Max Beerbohm	Stanley Weyman	
Myra Kelly	Stella Benson	
Nathaniel Hawthrone	Stella M. Francis	
Nicolo Machiavelli	Stephen Crane	
O. F. Walton	Stewart Edward White	
Oscar Wilde	Stijn Streuvels	
Owen Johnson	Swami Abhedananda	
P.G. Wodehouse	Swami Parmananda	
Paul and Mabel Thorne	T. S. Ackland